EKNATH EASWARAN

Eknath Easwaran (1910–1999) is respected around the world as an authentic guide to timeless wisdom, and as the originator of passage meditation, an eight-point program of universal spiritual practices that includes slowing down and one-pointed attention. In 1961 he founded the Blue Mountain Center of Meditation, which carries on his work with publications and retreats. His translations of the Indian spiritual classics are bestsellers in English, and more than 1.5 million of his books are in print.

A gifted teacher who lived for many years in the West, Easwaran lived what he taught, giving him enduring appeal as a teacher and author of deep insight and warmth.

W9-ASF-320

Our logo represents the ceremonial oil lamp used in homes and temples throughout Kerala, South India, where Eknath Easwaran was born and raised. "Little Lamp" is the pet name given to him by his maternal grandmother, his spiritual teacher.

Take Your Time

The Wisdom of Slowing Down

Eknath Easwaran

 NILGIRI PRESS

© 1994, 2006 by the Blue Mountain Center of Meditation
All rights reserved. Printed in Canada
Second edition. First printing August 2006

12 11 10 9 8 7 6 5

ISBN : 978–1–58638–095–3

Library of Congress Control Number: 2006928864

Publisher's Cataloging-in-Publication Data

Easwaran, Eknath.
Take your time : the wisdom of slowing down
/ Eknath Easwaran -- 2nd ed.
    p.   cm.
Includes index.
ISBN 978-1-58638-095-3 (pbk. : alk. paper)
1. Self-actualization (Psychology). 2. Time-management.
3. Interpersonal relations. 4. Conduct of life. I. Title
BF637.S4 E19 2006
640'.43-dc20   20006928864

Nilgiri Press is the publishing division of the Blue Mountain
Center of Meditation, a nonprofit organization founded by
Eknath Easwaran in 1961.
www.bmcm.org | info@bmcm.org
The Blue Mountain Center of Meditation
Box 256, Tomales, California 94971
Telephone: +1 707 878 2369 | 800 475 2369

Printed on FSC® paper

Table of Contents

This edition of *Take Your Time* incorporates revisions planned during the author's lifetime. In addition to minor changes, some dated references and stories have been removed or replaced by new material drawn from his talks, and the suggestions for practice have been set apart to encourage experimentation.

Most significantly, a new opening chapter drawn from previously unpublished work emphasizes the spiritual benefits of an unhurried mind and a more intentional life. *Take Your Time* was meant to complement books on time management so that juggling time and priorities can serve the need to find meaning and purpose in the affairs of everyday life. If other books help with to-do lists, *Take Your Time* aims at what one wants to *be*.

The Gift of Time

By Christine Easwaran

I had the privilege of knowing someone who had full possession of every moment – all the time there is. And he gave it away freely.

Time isn't a thing, of course. We can't really possess it or give it in the same way as we can give an object. When I say Eknath Easwaran had all the time there is, I mean that he lived completely in the present. Instead of being hurried by time, he was master of it.

Living in the moment is not the prerogative of mystics. It is prized by athletes, dancers, and other performing artists. Without warning, they tell us, they sometimes find themselves so absorbed in what they are doing that events slip into slow motion; time even seems to stop. They forget themselves, the

Christine Easwaran, wife of Eknath Easwaran, is president of the Blue Mountain Center of Meditation. She has been active in Easwaran's work since 1960.

limitations of the body and their everyday personality; there
is nothing but them and the ball, them and the music, them
and a vision too rarefied to be described. They are experiencing
"flow"; they are "in the zone."

Experiences like these, when one is lifted out of ordinary
time, are often accompanied by a sense of profound peace. Scientists explain this by brain chemistry, but to Easwaran,* brain
changes are effects. The cause, he explained, is that complete
absorption brings a healing pause in the frantic activity of the
mind. Whatever we are doing in that instant fills our consciousness. We are too absorbed to worry, to fret over the past or feel
anxious about the future, to be divided by conflicts or dwell on
what others might be thinking of us; we simply live. It's as if the
flickering of thoughts is our real clock: when it slows significantly, we are lifted into a higher level of awareness.

This is a precious clue, Easwaran tells us. It suggests that the
secret of fulfillment lies not outside us but in the way the mind
works. We may associate being "in the zone" with performances
like gymnastics or ballet, but activity is not what matters. What
these peak experiences teach us is that living in the moment is
a *mental* skill, a matter of training the mind – and that means it
can be learned. We don't have to be a star performer or rocket
scientist to learn this; it's within reach of all of us.

* *Easwaran* is his given name; *Eknath* is the name of his family, which is
matrilineal.

In this book, Easwaran offers ways to develop the skill of living in the present so that we can open up the promise held within each moment of our lives. The more we practice, the more we discover in the time we have – and so the nearer we move to having all the time in the world. That, Easwaran says, is our birthright as human beings. It has already been granted to us; we simply have to learn how to claim it.

When I met him in 1960, soon after his arrival in California as a professor from India on the Fulbright program, Easwaran was full to overflowing with the desire to teach these skills. A born teacher, he had distilled his experience into an eight-point program that he himself followed. In addition to his obligations at the University of California, he had speaking engagements throughout the Bay Area and even some popular lectures on campuses in Southern California.

The schedule was always tight, but he was never in a hurry. Not once, then or since, did I see him pressured into speeding up to get more done in the time available. By his example, he was constantly teaching what he knew from experience: the most effective way to accomplish a lot is to do one thing at a time and do it well.

The first time I remember Easwaran asking me to slow down was on a beautiful autumn afternoon in 1960. I was driving him back to Berkeley from Walnut Creek, where he had given an informal lecture on the philosophy of ancient India to a small but enthusiastic audience. The freeway was new and broad and there was almost no traffic. I had no reason to hurry, but under these conditions it was natural – and fun – to go the speed limit. So it came as a surprise to me when he asked me to slow down – I wasn't exceeding the limit, after all. But I dropped back anyway.

Yet habit is habit and the speedometer gradually worked its way back up.

Then he asked me the second time to slow down. This seemed ridiculous. I felt a little annoyed, as I had as a teenager when I was learning to drive on rural roads in Virginia and my dad would tell me the same thing. But then I remembered. This man is from India, where the pace of life is very slow. Why else would he want to go slow? So I slowed down.

This was my first lesson in slowing down. It took me a long time to understand why I should and much longer to learn how.

In those days, I simply couldn't understand why Easwaran placed so much importance on such matters. I thought it might be cultural. As an American, I took hurry for granted and considered it self-evident that speed means efficiency and faster is better. I soon learned that efficiency comes from complete concentration on one thing at a time, even when one has to manage several tasks. The secret is the unbroken flow of attention that characterizes peak performance.

Easwaran enjoyed watching sports – especially those he understood from playing them, such as tennis and soccer – because he enjoyed the concentration of a champion. I began to see that he too moved with the efficiency and grace of the performers he liked to watch. They understood the "inner game," he said; they knew the importance of the mind. That was his field, the mind. He wanted everyone to see that this training of the mind is the secret not just of first-rate tennis or ballet but of everything – of what he called the art of living – and that, just as in tennis or ballet, it could be learned. He was, if you like, everyone's personal trainer in the inner game of living.

The word "slow" is misleading when it implies sluggish. Easwaran was unhurried, but he was never sluggish. In an emergency he could act instantly, before those around him grasped what was happening. When planning was called for, however, he would often slow down like a gymnast poised before bursting into her routine. It was as if physical activity was a distraction at such times; everything important was happening deep inside. (I have read something very similar about Mahatma Gandhi.) Then, suddenly, he would act, still without hurry but with intense precision, setting in motion one by one the things that needed to be done.

Helping others to slow down occupied Easwaran's attention from the beginning of his career as a spiritual teacher until the end of his life. It was part of a message meant for the world, but nowhere seemed a better platform for delivering it than the United States.

In this book he describes the shock he felt on arriving in New York and seeing first-hand the pace at which Americans were moving. (Even then! Today 1959 seems leisurely.) That first day, he says, he decided never to get caught up in this kind of rat race – and not only that, but to help everyone around him to slow down too. At that point he was still putting the finishing touches on his Eight Point Program. Two of the points suddenly jumped in importance: slowing down and one-pointed attention, his term for doing one thing at a time with an undivided mind.

At first I don't think anyone listening to him understood why a spiritual teacher should place so much emphasis on anything so commonplace. Today it's clear that he was seeing what lay in store for our society if the pressures to hurry were not reduced. Thoughts are seeds, he explained; if cultivated, they have to grow into action and bear fruit with the passage of time. America was sowing the seeds of hurry; the fruit to come was all too clear.

The seventies brought the first signs of an adverse effect on health. *Type A Behavior and Your Heart* called attention to what Drs. Ray H. Rosenman and Meyer Friedman called "hurry sickness," a syndrome of time-driven behavior that they felt was closely associated with heart disease. Easwaran was especially pleased that their description included what they called "polyphasic thinking": not just trying to do many things in too little time, but trying to think about several things at once. At last, he felt, clinicians were looking at the role played by the mind.

Type A behavior syndrome is still debated by researchers, but Dr. Friedman's description fit so perfectly that it captured popular attention. "Type A behavior," he explained, "is above all a continuous struggle to accomplish more and more things in less and less time, frequently in the face of opposition – real or imagined – from other persons." Type A's are driven by an aggressive need to compete, and they keep score with anything that can be counted: how many facts they know, how much work they can do in an hour, how many things they can do at once.

When *Type A Behavior and Your Heart* was published, many Americans, as Jane Brody wrote recently in the *New York Times*, recognized in themselves "quite a few of the obnoxious – and perhaps life-threatening – traits typical of Type A behavior and vowed to make some changes." While researchers argued, Easwaran and I saw close friends who had undergone heart surgery transform their lives through Dr. Friedman's clinical program, which taught Type A's how to become Type B's – or, in Easwaran's language, how to slow down, learn to be more patient, and find meaning, love, and rich relationships in lives impoverished by years of hard driving in the fast lane. Dr. Friedman and his colleagues were demonstrating that even when time pressure is forced on us, we can learn to deal with it in freedom.

Yet life kept on getting faster. In the mid-eighties, *Time* magazine asked "Is America Running Out of Time?" in a cover feature full of warnings but short on suggestions for what to do. Newspaper and magazine articles talked about the hazards of "kids on the fast track," whose hurried lives and packed schedules mirrored those of their parents. Whenever Easwaran went out, he came back struck by how few people looked happy. Everyone was in a hurry – hurrying themselves, hurrying each other, hurrying their children. Therapist friends told us that each year they saw more clients complaining of the stress of a life with too much to do. Those who specialized in family counseling reported additional casualties: parents too busy to see each other, friendships slipping apart, children with stress disorders like those of executives.

Recently some thoughtful books on these themes have begun to appear, joining articles in business and women's magazines and even professional journals. Hurry is no longer "cool," no longer a mark of efficiency and success. And patience, thankfully, is beginning to be seen not as weakness but as a virtue that measures inner strength: the capacity not to be thrown off balance when things don't go our way. All these developments may be signs that our society is waking up to the toll that hurry and multitasking take not just on individual lives but on civilization itself.

I said that hurry was Easwaran's first concern on arriving in the US. It stayed with him to the end. In 1998, while he was in chronic pain, Easwaran agreed to give a talk at a local community college on a topic of his choice. In those days he rarely left home; when he did, it was only for a quiet drive. Nearing the end of his life, he had been giving all his time to retreat participants and close students, training those who would carry on after him.

Clearly this would be his last opportunity to address a wide audience. A topic of the utmost seriousness was called for. What did he want his message to be? Would he speak on meditation? Some theme from world mysticism? Mahatma Gandhi?

He chose to talk about slowing down. And he chose to use most of the time simply to tell stories, slipping in his characteristic touches of practical wisdom almost as asides.

In retrospect, I don't know why that should have been surprising. Wisdom has always been conveyed through stories. Stories are what we remember; they wrap ideals and values in images that stay with us all our lives. Great spiritual teachers consistently teach first by story and parable; explanations are dry by comparison.

So this is a book of stories. Again and again, as we read, we find ourselves in a familiar situation where we generally get impatient or upset – standing in line, waiting on hold, shopping with lively children who have agendas and timetables of their own. But as Easwaran relates each event, we see it through his eyes. From the perspective of an unhurried mind, familiar situations open up. We glimpse possibilities we had never suspected, little ways to change how we respond – and those little ways, as we act on them, quietly begin to transform our lives. An unhurried mind opens a door to discoveries in every moment. We don't have to change the circumstances around us; we simply need a mind that is quiet, calm, and kind.

I warmly invite you to step aside from the hurry around us, take your time, and let this gifted teacher help you discover a doorway to joy and serenity where most of us never think to look: in the ordinary activities of our everyday lives.

CHAPTER 1

Take Your Time

Every moment is a doorway
to meaning, purpose, and joy.
The key is an unhurried mind.

When our nieces Geetha and Meera were young, they lived with their grandmother, my mother, in a cottage that Christine and I shared. Even at seven, Geetha was a force to be reckoned with. She used to storm around like a small tornado as she got ready for school. That upset my mother, so one morning I decided to say something. "Geetha, dear," I urged her, "why don't you slow down? Take your time. You don't need to hurry."

"You can say that, Uncle," she shot back without breaking stride. "You don't have to go to school."

She had a point. All of us have to go to school one way or another, but rushing for the bus is no time to consider that we might actually get there just as well by slowing down – not just slowing down our physical movements, but especially a mind that is racing in overdrive trying to get things done.

It may sound paradoxical, but however tight our schedule, however many things clamor to be done, we don't need to hurry. If we can keep our mind calm and go about our business with undivided attention, we will not only accomplish more but we'll do a better job – and find ourselves more patient, more at peace.

> However much we have to do,
> we don't have to be in a hurry.

Our whole way of life militates against this today. Our civilization has developed a mania for speed, careening out of control in the fast lane of life – a race with no prize and no way of winning.

One sure sign is that no one has enough time. Another is how many of us are always hurrying to be late. Everyone seems to be trying to fit more and more into the same fixed twenty-four hours. That is the paradox: we hurry faster and faster only to find we have less and less time.

Have you noticed that when you try to fit more into a day, you're likely to go through the whole day late? Trying to squeeze more in, we only squeeze time out. The first thing we do each workday morning is check the clock; the rest of the day we're running to catch up. We grab breakfast without really seeing what is on the table, if we bother to sit down to a table at all. We barely taste the food or see the faces of those we live with.

And the pace accelerates. We dash for the bus or battle with rush-hour traffic and arrive at work – if nothing goes wrong – just in time. Not an extra minute to smile and say good morning, perhaps not even to see who else is in the office. They are not co-workers; they are specters getting in our way. And of course they feel the same. They have their own list of things to check off by the end of the day, and barely enough time to get them done if they can manage to fend off interruptions.

After a day of this, we are moving so fast that we can't change gears. We whip homeward like a boomerang. And we're *tired,* drained from the pace of it. We drop into a seat on the bus and close our eyes – and as we do, some mild-mannered chap next to us looks up from his paper and asks innocently, "What is that Australian creature with a three-letter name that ends in *u*?"

We don't want to be rude, but we hear our voice growl, "Emu!" The mind is screaming, "I don't care about crossword puzzles! Who cares about Australian creatures with three-letter names?" By the time we reach home, we're ready to blow up at the very next person we meet – who is, all too often, likely to be someone we love.

We don't have to live like this. People who are in control of their lives somehow manage to be on time without arriving hurried. They get things done without even getting flustered about it, while the rest of us, harried by the pressures of life, go from place to place always just a little late and slightly unprepared. We have forgotten that it is possible to go through the day without hurry, tending to each matter as it comes up without coming under pressure.

Living without hurry is a skill
that everyone can learn.

Living without hurry like this is not a gift; it is a skill. And that
means it can be learned. I began to learn it through the example
of Mahatma Gandhi, in whose India I grew up – and I might
add that I learned it when I *did* have to go to school, teaching
a full load of classes, managing a department, attending endless committee meetings, and keeping open hours for students
long into the evening, in addition to writing and lecturing over
All India Radio and a dozen other activities I enjoyed.

At that point in my career, I was a busy young man with a
packed schedule and quite a few irons in the fire. I had a job I
loved – teaching English literature – and was making a name
for myself in other fields. In graduate school I had even taken
an extra degree, in law as well as literature, because India had
just achieved independence and I was contemplating a career
in the foreign service. My generation was eagerly involved in
building a new nation. It was an exciting time, full of promise,
and everything seemed to be falling into my hands.

Yet for some reason it wasn't enough. I was busy, but there
was an emptiness in my heart that no success could fill. Something essential was slipping through my fingers. Meaning, perhaps. A sense of purpose, a reason for living. Certainly peace
of mind. I recalled a line from Thoreau: "It's not enough to be

busy. The question is, what are you busy about?" A good question. What did I want? I had been too busy even to ask.

In high school, I had read a story by H. G. Wells about a child who wanders down an unfamiliar street and spots a door in a plain white masonry wall. He opens it and discovers a garden where everything is welcoming and full of peace – a place where he belongs. The next day he tries to go back, but the door has disappeared.

Three or four times after that, as he grows into manhood and climbs the ladder of success, he turns a corner and happens to see the door again, just as he remembers it. He hesitates, but always he has something urgent to attend to and lets the moment go. The years pass and he attains fame and fortune, but he is haunted by regret that he never ventured through his door again.

When I read that story again in the middle of my life, I realized it applied to *me*. One detail that hadn't meant much when I was younger jumped out at me: every time that fellow sees his door in the wall again and decides to pass it by, he first looks at his watch. He can't take the time to stop to discover what he has always longed for.

In fact, the Buddha says, our constant hurrying is often a kind of anesthesia. It's not convenient to stop to ask big questions; it can even feel threatening. So long as we keep moving, we can put it off.

"Wake up!" the Buddha says. "It is time to wake up. Why do you go on sleeping?" I was almost forty; my alarm was ringing. It was time to step back, take a long view of my life, and reevaluate my priorities. What did I really want? What was life for?

I went about looking systematically. I knew several people I admired for their achievements; I knew others who were quite well off. I talked to them, but they couldn't help. Those with some self-knowledge even confided, "Don't look to me. I haven't found it either."

Being a professor, I went to the library and combed the stacks in every field that seemed relevant: psychology, philosophy, religion. I studied biographies of scientists and other luminaries who seemed to have found meaning and purpose for their lives. None of it shed light on how to live my own.

After a while of this, it occurred to me that I might be looking in the wrong places. With my university education, I had taken it for granted that people who had found fulfillment must be educated and successful. When I thought further, I realized that the people I knew who seemed happiest were often un-educated and unknown. I had grown up with them. They belonged to a way of life I had left behind and had no desire to return to, but their example told me that happiness had nothing to do with possessions, position, wealth, social status, or anything else outside.

A simple, unhurried life can be full of
wisdom and beauty.

I thought back to my childhood. Like the door in that story, it opened onto another way of life. My home state of Kerala is a green staircase on the southwest coast of India with a culture thousands of years old. Visitors are surprised at the beauty of the state and the independent, hardworking, simple way of life that most people there still follow. By modern standards, the village where I was born was backward: we had no electricity, no cinema, no radio, no police, no court of law. But the air was clean, the water pure; rainfall was abundant and the soil fertile. Our area was surplus-producing farmland; everything we needed was grown or produced in or near our village. We grew cereals, vegetables, and fruits; we grew the coconuts that supplied us not only with food but with fiber for ropes and oil that was extracted right in the village. All the artisans we needed – carpenters, blacksmiths, goldsmiths, potters, weavers – lived at hand.

Don't get the impression that this was a rustic life without artistry or beauty. South Indian classical music and dance have been perfected over thousands of years, and my father was a patron; we regularly enjoyed plays and concerts by some of the best performers in India. In those days, too, men who had left the village for professional careers often returned after retirement to make a contribution to the next generation, so two or three of my uncles taught subjects like Shakespeare and Sanskrit in our little school. I received an excellent education there, and a different kind of education from the land itself.

Of course, we didn't have cars then. A few had bicycles – I remember when my father pedaled the first one into our family compound – but most of us were happy to walk. It was not a chore; it was a source of simple delight. The roads were lined with trees: palms and banyans where we could see monkeys playing; mango and cashew trees that we boys liked to raid as we passed. And when I had to go to school, I didn't walk. Like little Geetha, I ran – but not out of hurry. I ran for the sheer joy of it. I ran to get there early so I could see my friends, and I ran home at noon to have my lunch hot from my mother's hands – and somehow, after eating, I managed to run back again in time for class.

I don't mean I lived in paradise. People in my village were subject to the same human foibles and discontents as everyone else. But despite the lack of telephones and automobiles, despite having to tell time by the sun instead of marching to efficient schedules by the clock, they were happy – happier, it seemed to me, than anyone I knew at my university. It was a precious clue. If a village teacher could be as happy as a cosmopolitan professor, fulfillment did not come from any particular activity, place, or circumstance. Perhaps it really could only be found within. Scarcely an original thought, but I had considered it only intellectually. Now it seized my heart.

> Fulfillment doesn't come from outside
> – we must look within ourselves.

From that perspective, one person in my village stood out like a beacon: my grandmother.

When I talk about Granny, I need to explain first that the branch of society I come from is rare in India as well as the rest of the world. It is a matriarchy, in which lineage is traced through the mother rather than the father and women have had legal rights for centuries. My grandmother was not the head of the family, but she was revered throughout the village for her wisdom. Whenever someone had a problem, he or she was likely to come to Granny.

Within the small orbit of this isolated village, hidden from the world among coconut palms and rice fields, my grandmother passed the whole of her seventy-odd years, participating fully in all aspects of village life. She arose daily with the morning star and worked till evening – sometimes, when necessary, well into the night, long after others had gone to bed.

She did everything carefully, giving each task her full attention without pressure or hurry, enjoying her work without ever being driven by it.

Granny often taught me with stories, and with the kind of short, pungent sayings that villagers live by throughout the world. "Your own gums are better than someone else's teeth," she would say whenever anyone in the family wanted to leave some responsibility to a servant. With that self-reliance went an independent spirit rare in rural India. Utterly unlettered, untraveled, uneducated, deeply rooted in an ancient way of life, she encouraged me to rebel against orthodoxy while she herself observed every ritual, ceremony, taboo, and sometimes ridiculous demand of a traditional society. When everyone else in my ancestral family was pressuring me to become an engineer, Granny just told me with quiet authority, "Follow your own star."

And she was completely fearless – another rare trait in a land where villagers live in fear of snakes, ghosts, disease, poverty, social disapproval, and countless other, nameless threats. In those days death was a familiar visitor, and in the center of our joint family home was a room called the "dark room" where the body of a person who had died was kept until it could be cremated. The candle in that room was not allowed to go out, which meant that someone had to stay with the corpse throughout the night. Most village Indians are terrified of ghosts, but for Granny, a corpse was just a tattered jacket that its wearer had discarded. On almost every occasion it was she who sat beside the body and kept the flame alive. "When Granny slept under our roof," one of my aunts told me, "we weren't afraid of anything."

That was what I wanted, I realized. That was the kind of person I wanted to be. But I didn't want her kind of life. Literature had opened unlimited vistas for me; I needed wide horizons. I wanted the best of both worlds: I wanted to combine my grandmother's inner strength and mastery with the modern, active life I had discovered for myself.

> Mahatma Gandhi showed how to face
> pressure without losing peace of mind.

I knew of one other person who was a master of pressures and priorities. Mahatma Gandhi had been an ideal for me since I visited him as a college student in the early thirties. As the leader of a nonviolent revolution involving four hundred million people, waged against the most powerful empire the world had yet seen, Gandhi was constantly under pressure. But it never seemed to touch him. On my first visit, at the height of India's struggle for independence, I caught him emerging from an all-day emergency meeting with the country's top leaders. Everyone else looked concerned and tense; Gandhi looked as relaxed as if he had been playing a game.

Today we think of Gandhi as the man who went about in sandals and homespun clothing even when invited to Buckingham Palace. But Gandhi was no simple villager. He had taken his law degree in London and was a wealthy, successful barrister when he began to dedicate his life and resources to public service. He was thoroughly acquainted with the realities of modern life.

It was a revelation to me, therefore, to see that this most practical of idealists knew the value of every minute. I don't think anyone has understood time better, or had a more intimate grasp of how a decision taken in a second can change the course of history. Unlike most of the rest of us in India, Gandhi considered it a mark not only of courtesy but of mastery to be on time wherever he went. Time was precious to him, other people were precious to him, so he treated their time and his own with the utmost respect. He wore only one piece of cloth around his waist and a second around his shoulders, but there was always a large pocket watch pinned to his waist with a safety pin. It was one of his noted eccentricities. And if anyone was late for an appointment, he would take this watch up and show it, no matter how distinguished his visitor. That was his gentle way of teaching us Indians to be on time.

Staying calm at the center enabled
Gandhi to accomplish great things.

Very few people in human history have accomplished more than Gandhi. Not many even had his vitality. If you look at some of his pictures, however, he appears as relaxed as a cat. Our cat Woosh sits at the foot of a tree so quietly that you think she is sleeping. Then, without warning, you see a blur of half a dozen cats in the air. Such an explosion of movement! I always wonder where all this energy comes from. She seems inert, but in action she becomes not one cat but half a dozen.

Gandhi was like that. When you looked at him, he seemed so quiet, so gentle, so mild, that it took a long time for the British to understand that just as a cat becomes half a dozen cats in the air, Gandhi became four hundred million human beings when he stirred the unconscious aspirations of the Indian people.

This is just the opposite of the time-driven personality, always on the go in an obsessive drive to achieve more and more in less and less time. Gandhi represents a different type, calm at the center but able to rouse a whirlwind of selfless action when the occasion demands. From the outside, such a person may look like an old Model T, but inside there is a Ferrari. How often we find people the other way around! A Ferrari body with a Model T engine. You see a lot of speed and flash but not much real progress, and no lasting contribution to the world.

Gandhi had not only a Ferrari engine but a Ferrari body as well. Only a strong, resilient body could have taken the rigors of that life. John Gunther, who was over six feet tall, recalled that he had to run to keep up with Gandhi when he went to interview him – and Gandhi was in his seventies at the time. His vigor was unmistakable. His power was untouched until the situation demanded it; then he would take off in no time, from zero to sixty in one minute, as calm as ever behind the wheel. It was all power steering, too. Seeing him gave me a whole new ideal of what it means to operate successfully in the modern world.

Even little incidents in Gandhi's life were a lesson to me. The first few times I had to stand before an audience in college, for example, my limbs would shake and the words would choke in my throat. It encouraged me greatly to learn that, as a law student, Gandhi too had been so acutely shy that he was unable even to read a brief introduction at a dinner party. He not only learned to overcome this shyness but spoke every day for most of his public life, often before some of the biggest and most hostile crowds you can imagine. But he was always relaxed and free from tension. There was no hurry, and he never succumbed to pressure.

One amusing instance of this has been preserved in the archives of radio. When Gandhi was in London in 1931 as a guest of the British government, he had become something of a celebrity in the United States, so CBS arranged a special transatlantic broadcast – a daring feat of technology in those days, when connections often failed. Everything was set up hours beforehand, and the radio and government people were wound tight with tension. Most of Gandhi's entourage was flustered too. A lot was at stake. It was important to them that Gandhi be effective in conveying his message to this large and influential audience.

Gandhi himself, however, didn't have any preparations to make. He had nothing to do with the arrangements; all he was expected to do was move the hearts of several million people in their native language when the time came. So he conducted his regular affairs in the midst of the confusion, waiting for his cue.

Finally a harassed-looking executive came over and said urgently, "Mr. Gandhi, the radio is ready for you. They are waiting in America!"

Gandhi sat down in front of the microphone and said, "You want me to speak into this?" Millions of people heard him, because he was already on the air. Everyone laughed as the speakers broadcast his words back into the room. The tension was broken, and Gandhi began to speak – with complete concentration, in no hurry, with total mastery of himself and the situation. You can still listen to the recording of that broadcast. It is one of the most moving speeches I have ever heard.

> An unhurried mind is calm, alert, and
> ready for anything.

My first visit to Gandhi had been prompted by one simple question: how had he done this? How had he managed to remake himself from a timid young law student with no purpose in life to a man so sure of himself that he could lead a nation without pressure, hurry, or fatigue? I found the answer that first evening. Gandhi had learned to live completely in the moment: whatever he did, he was one hundred percent present. And when I saw him absorbed in his evening meditation, I realized that complete absorption was the key.

I was still young then; it would be years before I was ready to learn how to apply the insights I gained that night. But gradually I understood that living completely in the present is the secret of an unhurried mind. When the mind is not rushing about in a hurry, it is calm, alert, and ready for anything. And a calm mind sees deeply, which opens the door to tremendous discoveries: rich relationships, excellence in work, a quiet sense of joy. It was a revelation. There was a door to the discovery of peace and meaning in every moment! All I needed to open it was a quiet mind.

I can't say I worked all this out at once. It took the shock of Gandhi's assassination and my grandmother's passing to realize that life was racing and I had no time to lose. But once I set my heart on learning this skill, I went about it with a passion. Without dropping anything from my academic career, I turned to meditation and worked out a systematic approach aimed at combining the active, creative, meaningful life I wanted with the mastery of mind I saw in Gandhi and my granny.

After a while, others around me became interested in what I was doing and asked to learn. Being a teacher, I made a method of it – an eight-point set of skills based on the practice of meditation.

I was putting the final touches on this Eight Point Program when I accepted a fellowship from the Fulbright exchange program to come to the United States. That turned out to be the beginning of a new career – not education for degrees, but education for living. Without realizing the implications, I was bringing my program to the pacesetters of the modern world.

CHAPTER 2

Slowing Down

*Eight ways to make the best of
the time we have every day.*

But nothing prepared me for New York. As soon as I disembarked I was surrounded by a ceaseless stream of traffic, a bewildering display of speed and noise. My first impression was of millions of cars flashing by. I thought there must be some race going on, with people racing for their lives. Was this the Daytona Beach I had read about? I could not understand why all these cars were rushing about like that.

Naturally, I assumed that once the sun set, the scene would quiet down. All those people would finally get wherever they were in such a hurry to get to and stagger out of their vehicles for a little rest.

There I had my second shock: the traffic continued even after the sun had disappeared. The peace and quiet of evening never came. Eight o'clock, nine o'clock, then ten . . . the traffic just went on and on. What seemed completely unnatural to me had become, to the people of New York, a way of life.

That very first day I made a conscious resolution never to get caught in that kind of race.

"The pace of life here *is* fast," friends reassured me. "But don't worry; you'll adjust."

I replied, "I don't want to adjust. And not only that, I want to help everyone around me to get out of the rat race too."

I have lived in this country for over thirty years now, and I have kept my resolve. Not once have I let myself be hurried by the pace of life here, no matter how severe the pressures around me. And I am proud to say that in the years since then, I have helped thousands of people to slow down too. From that experience has come this book.

> Just one person slowing down helps
> everyone around to relax too.

During my first Christmas in California, I went to the post office to send a package to my mother in India. As I neared the sedate old building, erected in a time when the pace of life was slower, I noticed cars double-parked and people darting up and down the broad granite steps. Inside was a scene of frustration, exasperation, and sometimes outright anger.

Crowd or no crowd, I needed to mail my package. I joined a long queue and stood patiently watching the scene around me. Everyone was giving unintended lessons in how to put yourself under pressure. One fellow in front of me was bouncing up and down as if he were on a pogo stick. He was in such a hurry that he just had to release his nervous energy somehow, and with people pressing you in front and behind, the only direction possible is up.

The gentleman in back of me was also in a hurry, and he was expending his nervous energy by blowing hot air down my neck.

"Well," I thought, "Christmas is the time for expressions of good will." So I turned around. "Please take my place," I told him. "I'm not in a hurry."

He was so distracted that he didn't hear me. He just said brusquely, "What?"

"Take my place," I repeated. "I have time. I'm in no hurry at all."

He stared, and then he began to relax. I felt the atmosphere around us begin to change. He apologized for being in such a hurry and mumbled something about being double-parked. I wanted to ask, "Why do you double-park?" But I thought better of it.

Slowly the queue moved forward. The young woman at the counter was probably a college student filling in for the holidays, and she was making mistake after mistake – giving the wrong stamps, giving the wrong change – while people complained and corrected her. I could see that she was getting more and more upset; and the more upset she got, the more mistakes she made and the longer each transaction took. All because everybody was in a hurry! If the scene had ever had any Christmas cheer, it was evaporating rapidly.

I'm fond of students; I was a professor for many years. So when it came my turn at the window, I said, "I'm from India. Take your time."

She looked as if she couldn't believe it. But she smiled and relaxed, and she gave me the right change and the right stamps too. I thanked her and wished her a merry Christmas.

As I walked out, I noticed that the man behind me returned her smile. The whole room had relaxed a little; I even heard a ripple of laughter from the end of the queue. Pressure is contagious, but so is good will. Just one person slowing down, one person not putting others under pressure, helps everyone else to relax too.

To paraphrase the Buddha, we learn to do this by doing it. We learn to slow down by trying to slow down. This chapter will give you some ways to start – ways I learned in the hectic days of my university teaching career. The suggestions that follow are not catch-all solutions. They are skills and grow through practice. The more you apply them, the more opportunities you will find to apply them further.

1. Give Yourself More Time

The easiest way to find more time is so simple that we often overlook it: get up earlier.

This does much more than simply gain another hour or so of clock time. The pace you set first thing in the morning is likely to stay with you through the day. If you get up early and set a calm, unhurried pace, it is much easier to resist getting speeded up later on as the pressures of the day close in on you.

This simple step has profound effects. In the natural rhythms of life, there is a period in the junctions between night and day, in the ebb and flow between activity and rest, when the mind grows calm. If you set aside a period of quiet time early in the morning, it puts your activities into a more peaceful perspective that will stay with you all day.

Then, if at all possible, have a leisurely breakfast with family or friends before going off to work. If you live alone, it is still helpful to sit down with a nourishing breakfast – don't eat it standing up! – and enjoy it without hurry. All these things set the pace you will be following for the rest of the day – and, to the extent they become habits, for the rest of your life.

Similarly, get to work a little early – in time to speak to those you work with, in time for a few minutes of reflection while you arrange the priorities that face you at work. These are simple steps, but they can go a long way in slowing down the pace of life, not only for you but for those around you as well.

At the University of Minnesota, where the Fulbright program first posted me, I used to go to the cafeteria at seven-thirty in the morning, when it opened, and sit down to enjoy a leisurely breakfast. At about ten to eight the doors would burst open and the students would come pouring in by the hundreds, sweeping through the cafeteria line. They would alight briefly at the table, inhale their food, and in ten minutes they would all be gone – off to their eight o'clock classes. It never failed to astound me.

Finally, one morning I stopped a student I knew and asked him, "Tell me, why do you come for breakfast at ten to eight?"

He was really embarrassed at my simplicity. "Because," he explained, "I get up at a quarter to eight."

When we start the day with just minutes for breakfast, we are going to be rushing all day long.

2. Don't Crowd Your Day

The desire to fit too much into a fixed span of time is pervasive, and technology merely adds to the pressure. We are expected to keep up with more and more information at work and at home, and the media obligingly drown us in it. I know people who feel duty-bound to read it, too. After all, some of it *must* be important. We really ought to know what's in it . . .

Often we cope with this by trying to skim through everything that comes our way. It is a race – like so much else in our lives. But is it a race we want to participate in? When we feel robbed of time already, do we want to spend what little we have on activities that only add to the noise and clutter in the mind?

To relieve this pressure, we simply have to stop trying to do everything possible. It is important to realize that we can't read everything, can't keep ourselves entertained every available moment, can't absorb or even catch all the so-called information that is offered to us every day. We have to make choices – which requires an unhurried mind.

Make wise choices about what you read. Read only what is necessary or worthwhile. And then take the time to read carefully.

I have always loved to read. I grew up appreciating Carlyle's statement that "a good book is the purest essence of a human soul." Even as a student I would seek out something truly worth reading and read it slowly, with complete attention, so as to absorb all the author had poured into it. Even today I don't like background music or a cup of coffee at my side. And when I reach the end of a chapter or a section, I close the book and reflect on what I have read. I would much rather read one good book with concentration and understanding than to skim through a list of best-sellers that will have no effect on my life or my understanding of life. One book read with concentration and reflected upon is worth a hundred flashed through without any absorption at all.

Trying to read everything that comes our way is just another aspect of trying to do it all. With television, the equivalent is channel surfing. Once we have learned there is nothing worth watching, why not turn it off? Flitting through fifty or more channels just divides attention even more. And when we can't get our mind to slow down enough to stay on the same focus, how can we expect to enjoy anything? How can we do a good job at anything we do?

Because our lives are so fast, we take a short attention span for granted. A truly creative mind has a very long attention span. When a great painter, musician, or scientist turns to a subject, he or she stays with it not for minutes but for hours, days, and even years, going deeper and deeper.

It's not only with ourselves that we try to squeeze more and more into our lives. We do so with the lives of those we love as well. Many parents I know spend hours each day ferrying children to after-school activities. I am all for giving children opportunities, but even here we need to be selective – perhaps especially here, because children have little control of their own time. Their time is in our hands.

Parents today feel children are deprived if they do not have a variety of activities. But this simply isn't so. Children are deprived if they don't have their parents' love and attention, they are deprived if they don't have food and fresh air and a good education and time for play, but they really lose very little if they are not kept moving from Scout meeting to soccer practice to piano lessons to karate. Even more than adults, children need to be protected from the pressure to hurry. When we fill their days like this, we are only teaching them to hurry, hurry, hurry as we do.

3. Ask What's Important

Long ago, when I began to see the benefits of meditation, I wanted to be sure I made time for it every day. But I couldn't see how I could fit it in. I had an extremely busy schedule, with responsibilities from early morning until late at night.

I valued all this, but I was determined to make meditation a top priority. So I sat down and made a list of all the things I felt bound to do.

Then I took my red pencil and crossed out everything that was not actually necessary or beneficial. Some of the results surprised me. I found I had been involved in activities that I couldn't honestly say benefited anyone, including myself. I had simply become used to doing them. When I surveyed what remained, I found I had freed a number of hours every week.

This red-pencil exercise may seem painful, but very quickly you will find it liberating. You will find you have more time to do the things that are important to you, more time for family and friends, more time for everything that makes life worthwhile.

Of course, this list reflects *your* priorities, no one else's. No one will be looking over your shoulder while you decide what gets the red pencil. And, of course, the list is not permanent. Every now and then I still repeat this exercise, making a list and questioning all my activities because priorities change.

One of the most important things about this kind of review is that it is an admission to yourself that you can't do everything. Once you make this realization, you can begin to ask, "What do I want to do? What is important?" When all is said and done, if you don't make this list for yourself, the pressures of everyday life will simply make it for you.

When you have pared down your list, test your decision for a few weeks. Often you will find that you and the world can do without activities you had thought essential, and that you have all kinds of new time to allocate as you choose.

When I first did this, I found to my surprise that quite a few of the things I had been engaged in were actually expendable. I had never suspected this. When I dropped out of these activities, I was under the impression that people would miss me. I even asked myself what I would do when people asked why I hadn't been turning up. I was rather embarrassed to discover that nobody noticed my absence. Nobody even asked, "Where have you been?" It was a very healthy reminder.

4. Take Time for Relationships

Personal relationships are often the first casualties in a speeded-up way of life.

"Take time for relationships" may sound like odd advice. I have just suggested freeing time, and now I'm saying to give more time to others. And it's true that relationships require time – sometimes a good deal of time. But it is time well spent.

Take the simple question of meals. As the pace of life has accelerated, a great many of us have got out of the habit of sitting together and sharing a leisurely meal with family or friends. Often we eat alone, in a hurry, on our feet, even on the run or behind the wheel. I know people who seldom really eat a meal at all; they forage, or string together a series of snacks. This is not only the result of hurry, it adds to it. We can slow down by taking the time – *making* the time – to find a friend or two and create a little oasis in our day where we can shut out the pressures around us and enjoy human company.

Eating together is considered a sacrament in many cultures. These simple bonds play a part in holding a society together. So even if you live alone, arrange to share a meal regularly with friends or family. I know people who live alone through choice, but who carefully maintain and nurture personal relationships by getting together with friends to prepare and enjoy meals. It is not only nutrition you are getting when you do this, but also the loving companionship shared by everyone at the table.

Personal relationships, of course, not only take time, they take "quality time." This is especially true with children, where what matters is not only the number of hours we spend but also the attention we give, the love we show, the extent to which we enter into the child's world instead of dragging him or her into our own. Schedules are fine at the office, but children have a sense of time that is very different – and much more natural. They don't know about appointments and parking meters and living in the fast lane, and we cannot make them understand. All we can do is hurry them along.

We adults can learn to slow down enough to enter their world; it's not their job to speed up and join ours. Where is the hurry? What period of life is more precious than childhood? If we understood its worth, we would devote ourselves to slowing down the pace of childhood instead of rushing our children out of it. The time we spend on our children while they are young will be more than repaid when they reach their teenage years.

5. Take Time for Reflection

Taking time to pause and reflect now and then is not only part of slowing down; it is one of the rewards, too. And because it adds to efficiency and effectiveness in any walk of life, it is a very good use of time.

Of course, there are situations when immediate action is

required, when there is no time to pause and think. But such situations are rare, and the best way to prepare for them is to learn to stay calm and pause to think when circumstances are pressuring us to hurry.

This skill is applicable everywhere. I can give one example from my university, where final examinations observed the time limit to the minute. This naturally put students under a good deal of pressure, and most of them would start writing the moment the examination paper was put in their hands. But there were always a few who would pause to study the choice of essays, choose the ones they could answer best, and plan their time; only then would they begin to write. And generally they would do well – often better than a brighter student who plunged in to answer without thinking.

Whether it is an exam, a report at work, or even just a reply to a letter, it always helps to stop and reflect over what we need to say. We need to remind ourselves to take the time for reflection, for observation, for original thinking.

6. Don't Let Yourself Get Hurried

Often, after hearing me talk about slowing down, someone will come up and say, "What you say sounds good, but you don't know my job situation. I have to hurry."

Job requirements do vary, yet I have been told by an emergency medical technician doing ambulance work that it is possible to resist being hurried even in the midst of frantic circumstances. In fact, he said, that is just when he needs to keep his mind cool, concentrated, and clear. In such situations, the hands and brain of a paramedic or nurse or firefighter have been highly trained. They know what to do, and they carry out their duties swiftly. A speeded-up mind only gets in the way. (In later chapters I will give you some effective techniques for staying slow and concentrated when people are trying to speed you up.)

Second, with some reflection, it is possible to avoid a great many situations where we know we are going to be pressured to speed up. If we look at our home life and our work, we may see that a surprising number of these situations can be forestalled. If we cannot avoid these circumstances, it helps to be forewarned. Eventually, we may find ways of escaping a predicament in which we thought we had no choice.

Hurry is built into our culture; the more you look, the more instances you will see. Look at the amount of time we are granted by traffic lights to cross a busy street. The first time I encountered this phenomenon, I waited dutifully at the corner until the sign flashed "Walk" and then stepped off the curb. When I was halfway across, it suddenly commanded: "Wait!" I wanted to object, "I haven't crossed yet! If you want me to stop on this busy street, I'm not likely to make it home in one piece."

I see people hurry to cross streets now before the light changes, dragging little children behind them. I remember one old man holding up a pleading hand as he tried to hurry, as if to beg the cars not to run over him. I can imagine the day when the signal will say "Wait" and then, more honestly, "Run!" And we will obey, sprinting across in the unquestioned belief that it is right for us to be so hurried.

7. Cultivate Patience

Patience is one of life's unsung virtues. When people write about love, they use capital letters, italics, and calligraphy; everybody gives love the red-carpet treatment. But where patience is concerned, who cares? Nobody writes poems about patience. There are no popular songs about it. If the word does make an appearance, it is only because it contains two syllables and fits the meter.

This is unfair, because patience is the very heart of love. I don't think any skill in life is more valuable. Patience is the best insurance I know against all kinds of emotional and physical problems – and it is absolutely essential for learning to slow down.

Very few people are born with patience, but everyone can learn to develop it. As with slowing down, all we have to do is try to be patient every time life challenges us. And there are many, many opportunities to practice every day.

This doesn't require a gigantic canvas. Mogul art, one of the highlights of artistic achievement in India, often is in minia-ture. The artist concentrated on very small areas, working with such tenderness and precision that one has to look carefully to see the love and labor that has gone into it. Living is like Mogul art: the canvas is so small and the skill required so great that it's easy to overlook the potentialities for artistry and love.

One beautiful, balmy Sunday soon after my mother and nieces arrived from India, Christine and I took them out for ice cream. I rode in the back of our VW bus with Meera on one side and Geetha on the other. They chatted gaily the whole way, without a break, asking me all kinds of questions. I kept reminding myself of what most of us older people forget: that every child has a point of view. They have their own way of looking at life which makes them ask these questions, and for them, things like why *Texaco* and *Mexico* should be spelled differently when the endings rhyme are matters of vital importance.

When we got to town, we had to walk slowly because my mother was almost eighty. The children, however, wanted to run – and they wanted me to join them. I didn't say, "It's not proper for a pompous professor to be running about. It takes away from his pomp." Instead, I made a good dash for it. I thought I would meet with appreciation, but little Geetha just objected, "You're not supposed to step on the lines." There was no "thank you," no "well done"; I had to do it all again.

Geetha had just learned to read, so when we reached the ice cream parlor she stood staring at the big board. "What are all those flavors?"

I protested, "There are over a hundred!"

She tried to read a few and then asked, "What is that long word I can't read?"

I said, "Pistachio."

"That's my flavor." So she got that, double dip, and Meera got butter brickle.

They nursed their cones all the way home. I was in the back seat between them again, and every now and then they would exchange licks – across my lap. My first impulse was to warn, "Don't drip on me!" Then I reminded myself that from their point of view, ice cream is much more important than clothes. We made it home without incident, with the girls and my mother laughing happily about a perfect day.

We learn patience by practicing it, the Buddha says. What better way than by sharing time with children at their own pace and seeing life through their eyes?

8. Slow Down Your Mind

This is the real crux of slowing down: developing an unhurried mind.

In India I had the privilege of meeting a Sufi teacher whose name is known around the world today: Meher Baba. The key to his message was expressed in simple, memorable words: "A mind that is fast is sick. A mind that is slow is sound. A mind that is still is divine."

This quiet statement, so apparently out of step with the modern world, is not only wise but extremely practical. To make it intelligible, I like to compare the mind with something familiar: television.

Imagine your mind as a kind of television with thoughts constantly changing channels. In this case, however, the remote control device is out of your hands – the mind changes channels on its own. When a thought succeeds in holding your attention, your mind is settling on a particular show. But when you get speeded up, the mind is racing through split-second shots like a rock music video.

Destructive thoughts like fear and anger tend to be fast. If we could see the mind when it is caught in such thoughts, we would see thoughts tumbling over each other so fast that we don't know what we are thinking.

That is why anger has such a dramatic effect on the body. The next time you get angry, check your vital signs; you will notice your breathing in a race with your heart. You breathe faster and faster, the heart beats faster and faster; stress hormones get pumped into your system to prepare you for fight or flight. When I see somebody in a fury, I see it as one-thousandth of a heart attack. No amount of nutrition and exercise can protect us against the ravages of an untrained mind.

The more we slow down the thinking process, the more control we have over our lives. That is why Meher Baba says a mind that is slow is sound. When your mind stops racing, it is naturally concentrated rather than distracted, naturally kind instead of rude, naturally loving instead of selfish. That is simply the dynamics of the mind.

People who don't easily get provoked, even when there is cause for provocation, don't "fly off the handle." It's difficult to upset them, difficult to speed up their minds. They can stay calm in the midst of pressure, remain sensitive to the needs of all involved, see clearly, and act decisively. During a crisis – from a minor emergency at the office to a major earthquake – such people help everyone else to stay clearheaded. They are protecting not only themselves from danger, but those around them too.

The Buddha called this "living intentionally." It is a way of life. Slowing down is not the goal; it is the means to an end. The goal is living in freedom – freedom from the pressures of hurry, from the distractions that fragment our time and creativity and love. Ultimately, it means living at the deepest level of our awareness.

An unhurried mind brings the capacity to make wise choices every day – choices of how we use our time, of where we place our resources and our love. I am not just talking about avoiding the rat race, but about a life full of an artistic beauty – a life that has almost vanished from modern civilization, but is quite within the reach of everyone.

In this, I believe, we do more than simply elevate our own personal lives. We begin to remake our civilization. We can begin to transform our global jungle into a real global village, where our children will remember naturally the needs of all the children on the face of the earth. This is our destiny. This is what we were all born for and what we have been looking for all of our lives, whatever else we have been seeking.

Ideas and Suggestions

Experiment with getting up a little earlier each day. Use the time you gain for getting a more relaxed start on the day: more time for breakfast, a few minutes' walk, or reading something inspirational. Avoid the temptation to check e-mail, catch up on the news, or anything else that you know just adds to the pressure or speeds you up.

Try controlling your own "information overload." What do you really have to read? Can you watch less TV or set a limit to Internet browsing? Experiment and keep track of the results.

Try the "red pencil" exercise on pages 44–45.

Meals are a great time for giving relationships a more important place in your day. If you often eat alone, find a friend to share lunch with. Give yourselves enough time not to hurry – and avoid talking business!

Set aside a regular time for reflection. A weekend morning, before the day gets started, is a good way to begin. You might use the time for thinking about what's really important to you in the long run – a "Lifetime To Do" list, or even a "To Be" list.

See if you can find a situation where you're regularly pressured to speed up. Can you think of a way to forestall it, perhaps by starting earlier or rearranging your time? If you can break the pattern, you've made a major gain in what the Buddha calls "intentional living."

Practice patience – make a game of it. Make a date to do something special with a small child or two and go at their pace, see through their eyes, enjoy their enjoyment.

When you catch yourself getting angry, observe your mind; see if you can catch it beginning to speed up. If you're feeling adventurous, try to step back a little rather than react. (At this point, you're just learning to observe your mind; there will be specific techniques to try in later chapters.)

CHAPTER 3

One Thing at a Time

Even when we have a lot to do,
we can avoid stress and hurry
by tackling one thing at a time.

Most of us have times when the mind starts
playing one of its old tapes – "He did this to me; she said that
to me" – and just won't be switched off. Our emotions can get
so stirred up that we cannot sleep, we cannot eat, we cannot let
that memory go.

At such times, the skill we need is the ability to turn our
attention completely away from that old incident – to withdraw
attention from the past and bring it back to the present.

I have talked to people caught in old resentments like this
and tried to console them. "When did this quarrel take place?"

They answer glumly, "Seven years ago. In Minneapolis."

I remind them, "That's seven years and two thousand miles
away from here and now."

It is not an incident in the past that agitates our mind at times
like these. It is the attention we give the thought of that incident now. The more attention, the bigger the incident appears.
Without attention, it is simply a ghost from the past.

That is why the training of attention is such an important

part of bringing the mind to a calmer, more peaceful state. Along with slowing down, we need to learn how to keep our mind focused – and one of the most effective ways to learn this is to do, with complete attention, only one thing at a time.

> When the mind is uncontrolled, we
> don't think our thoughts – our thoughts
> think us.

Trying to get through life without control over your attention is a little like trying to reach a destination with no control over your car.

Suppose you leave work at five as usual, get in your car, and head for home. It is a beautiful day, and you are enjoying the view and the unusually light traffic when suddenly, without warning, your car swerves into the right-hand lane. You grab the wheel sharply, but the car ignores you and pulls off onto the next exit. In horror, you realize that you are not driving your Ford any more. It is driving you – it has a mind of its own.

You want to go home, but your car has other ideas. It finds the town tempting. You start to panic. What is the matter with this car?

After a desperate struggle, you manage to get back on the highway. But soon you feel that irresistible tug on the wheel. The car takes over once more, pulling to get off the road. After fighting with you for a few exits, it gets its way and careens off at Paradise Drive. The malls on both sides of the road are full of shops; your Ford seems fascinated by window-shopping. But you don't care; all you want is to get back on the highway again.

It's a fight like this all the way home. When you finally arrive, three or four excursions later, you're out of gas and late for dinner. Where did the time go? Who was in control?

A story like this belongs in the realm of science fiction, but when it comes to our attention, we often have as little control as the driver of this car. With temptations and distractions on every side, we are used to the mind weaving all over the road, swerving from lane to lane and causing danger to ourselves and everyone around us.

The next time you wash the dinner dishes, for example, see how many times your thoughts wander in just fifteen minutes. You may catch your mind straying to the quarrel you had last week over some absurd little disagreement. It flickers back to the pan you are scrubbing, but only for a moment; then it is off again.

Now the suds remind you of snow, and your unruly thoughts wander back to Christmases past. A few lines of "I'm Dreaming of a White Christmas" float through your mind. You are no longer standing in front of a sink in California; you are two thousand miles away in the depths of a Minnesota winter.

From dishes in California to snows in Minnesota – this happens in the thinking process of everybody. We like to say we were thinking those thoughts, but it would be more accurate to say our thoughts think us because we have so little control over them.

Directing attention at will is the most
precious skill in life.

Fortunately, we don't have to put up with this. Attention can be
trained, and no skill in life is greater than the capacity to direct
our attention at will.

The benefits of this are numerous. If you have trained your
mind to give complete attention to one thing at a time, you can
achieve your goal in any walk of life. Whether it is science or the
arts or sports or a profession, concentration is a basic require-
ment in every field. And complete concentration is genius.

I have a friend who is an excellent driver with a first-rate car.
On a long-distance trip she glides smoothly into the through
lane and cruises straight to her destination without even changing lanes. She never seems to exert herself, and she always manages to think a little ahead. Streams of traffic just part like the
Red Sea before Moses to let her through. And her concentration is like that too. When she is behind the wheel, her mind is
steady and her attention never wavers.

This kind of one-pointed attention is helpful in whatever
job you are doing. But perhaps the greatest benefit is the emotional stability it brings. In order to get angry, your concentration must be broken – your mind has to change lanes. In order
to get afraid, your mind has to change lanes. In order to get
upset, your mind has to change lanes. It is not that you choose
to let your attention wander; your mind simply takes over and
changes whether you want it to or not. If you can keep your
mind in one lane, your concentration is unbroken; you are

master of your attention. Whatever the circumstances, whatever the challenges, you will not lose your sovereignty over
your thinking process.

A wandering mind is not just a modern problem. Even in
the days of the Compassionate Buddha, more than twenty-five
hundred years ago, people used to complain to him, "I have
problems at home. I have problems at work. I can't sleep well; I
can't eat well; I am always upset."

The Buddha would look at them with his wise eyes and say,
"Nobody is upsetting you. Nothing is upsetting you. You get
upset because you are upsettable."

Then he would add, "Don't you want to be unupsettable?"

"Yes, Blessed One."

"Don't you want to be happy?"

"Of course, Blessed One."

"Then," he would say, "you have to train your mind."

That is what we all yearn for – a mind that cannot be upset
by anything. And we can achieve it, too, but it calls for a lot of
work in the training of attention.

The Buddha was perhaps the most acute psychologist the
world has seen, because he understood the workings of the
mind from the inside. When we have resentments or hostilities or ill will, he would say, not only our attention but our vital
energy is caught in the past. When we learn to recall attention
from the past and keep it completely in the present, we reclaim
a tremendous reserve of vital energy that has been trapped in
the past like a dinosaur. Every time we do this, we restore a little more of our vital wealth to the present moment.

Just as all of us carry the burden of resentments from the past, we all have fears and anxieties related to the future. This is part of our conditioning as human beings. But here, too, we can learn to prevent our energy from wandering into the future and keep it completely in the present.

In the long run – I am anticipating many years of training attention – you won't think about the past at all. It is not that you cannot remember the past; you just don't think about it. You won't think about the future, either: not that you don't plan for the future, but you are not entangled in what it will bring. You live one hundred percent in the present – which means you are one hundred percent alive.

> When we live one hundred percent
> in the present, we are one hundred
> percent alive.

Until it is trained, the mind will continue to go its own way, because it is the nature of an untrained mind to wander. If your mind were to appear on one of those late-night television talk shows, the host would ask it, "Why do you keep wandering like this?"

And the mind would say, "I never got an education! I never got sent to school. Everybody says to me, 'It's a free world. Do what you like.'"

That is why all of us have wandering minds: it is simply lack of training. But just as any great physical skill – tennis, soccer, gymnastics, skiing, skating – is acquired, through persistent practice under the guidance of an experienced coach, we can learn to train the mind.

When we are listening to a lecture or reading a book on slowing down, how is it that strange, irrelevant thoughts arise – thoughts about a restaurant that has just opened, or the new swimming pool, or what we will do if we win the lottery? After all, what we want is to listen or read with complete attention; we're not encouraging extraneous thoughts to arise. Nonetheless, here they are: thoughts of the most unexpected kind, barging in without so much as a knock on the door.

To some extent, I absorbed the skill of one-pointed attention rather early in life. My grandmother, my spiritual teacher, was constantly teaching me in many little ways – especially by her personal example – to do one thing at a time.

I will always remember sitting down one morning to my usual breakfast of rice cakes and coconut chutney, which my grandmother prepared to perfection. I was so partial to this combination that on one occasion I ate twelve rice cakes in a sitting.

On this particular morning, however, I had got absorbed in a book by Washington Irving. I had discovered the delightful story of Rip Van Winkle, a fellow who could sleep for twenty years. I was holding the book with my left hand and reading while my right hand would take a rice cake, dip it in the chutney, and put it into my mouth.

Even then, my capacity for concentration was rather good. And I loved a good book. So I must have been immersed in the adventures of Rip Van Winkle for some time before I noticed that there was nothing in my right hand and nothing was going into my mouth. I turned to look and saw that the plate was gone, the rice cakes were gone, the chutney was gone. I had just been moving an empty hand to my mouth.

I was indignant. "Who took my rice cakes away?" I demanded.

"You weren't even tasting them," my granny said. "You were reading. You didn't even know I took them away. That is poor reading and poor eating." She wouldn't give me my breakfast until I had put the book away.

Doing something else while we eat is such a common habit today that no one even questions it. If you go to a restaurant in the business district at lunchtime, you will see any number of hurried executives lunching off the *Wall Street Journal.* You can watch as one morsel of salad is consumed and then one morsel of *Journal.* That is poor eating and poor business practice, too. If I were to select a stockbroker, I would try to find one who knows how to keep his concentration on salad when he is eating salad and on the *Wall Street Journal* when he is planning my investments.

Much more alarming, I see people talking on the phone while they drive. They say, "You can call me anytime, anywhere." As if this were an advantage! Imagine, they never have a moment when they can be sure they won't be interrupted – not while they are driving, not even while they are walking down the street. In fact, such inventions as cell phones and computers actually encourage our tendency to do two or more things at once.

For students, the practice of one-pointed attention is essential. Complete concentration is necessary for learning. But go to any university and see how many students are doing two or more things at a time – listening to music, drinking coffee, smoking, talking, and then trying to study at the same time. When the time comes for a grade, they are likely to get Incomplete – a grade that seems perfect for divided attention.

If you have a concentrated mind, you will find that you won't need as many hours to learn new skills or comprehend difficult material. It saves a lot of time, and it will give you valuable self-assurance whenever you have to master something new.

One-pointed attention is most rewarding in personal relationships.

One-pointed attention is most rewarding in personal relationships, where nothing can be more important than giving complete attention to one another.

This is particularly true with children. Children naturally ask all kinds of questions and take a long time to tell their stories, and in millions of homes the parents are doing something else as they reply, "Yes, yes, I see." And in millions of homes, the parents are surprised when their children don't listen to them.

Those little bright eyes know when your attention is wandering. When they are telling you the news from school, give your full attention. Everything else can be set aside for the moment. You are teaching your children to listen to you.

That is how I was taught by my grandmother and my mother. Every day, when I came back from school, my grandmother would say, "Tell me everything from the time you left home until the time you came back." All my news was important to her. She gave me her undivided attention as I went through the events of the day from English class through the soccer game and the swim in the river after school. Children need this kind of attention, and we need time for listening to their stories. Our undivided attention is more precious to them than any gift we could buy them.

> Every conversation is an opportunity
> for learning to be one-pointed.

In Zen, they say that when you are listening to the roshi, the Zen master, your eyes should not wander even for a moment. I think that is good advice for any occasion. When somebody is talking to you, give your full attention. Eyes, ears, mind, and heart should be focused on the person you are listening to. He or she can't help responding to your wholehearted attention. Every conversation is an opportunity for training the mind to be one-pointed.

I can't help but notice how common the opposite is. Watch people at a social gathering. How many are really giving their full attention to the person they are talking with? There may be a lot of animated conversation and an air of conviviality in the room, but if you observe carefully, you will see that most people's eyes are wandering – which means their minds are wandering too. If you can't keep your attention in one place, how can anything not be boring? Nothing can be interesting, after all, unless you give it your attention.

Effortless concentration is the secret of all personal relationships, whether it is with casual acquaintances, co-workers, colleagues, friends, or family. And when relationships are not particularly cordial, one-pointed attention is even more important. It is an exceptional person who can give complete attention to somebody who is being unpleasant, but when you can do this, you can slowly disarm even a hostile person simply by listening without hostility, with complete and even loving attention. In my own long experience, no thrill is greater than that of winning over a tough opponent to be an ally.

> Every time we are criticized,
> we have an opportunity to grow.

In life we are going to come across opposition everywhere, especially when we are doing original, worthwhile work. Instead of becoming resentful or afraid, we can learn to look upon every opponent as a possible supporter and every piece of criticism as a way to grow. These are the challenges we need in order to learn how to win over opposition, to turn a difficult situation into an opportunity, and to transform our own negative qualities into strengths.

I vividly remember watching one of the best tennis matches I have ever seen: a sustained fight in which every play was countered by one of equal skill. I kept telling my friends, "I don't care who wins. It is of no consequence to me who gets the cup and who doesn't. What I enjoy is seeing these great players equally challenged, because it brings out the best in each of them." That is how I see life: not somebody winning and somebody else losing, but each of us growing as difficulties and challenges draw us up to our best.

When you see opposition, therefore, do not get afraid. If you can keep your concentration unbroken, you can look on tough opposition as a challenge to test your capacities, so that through patience, courtesy, and the depth of your conviction, you can win over even the fiercest opponent.

All this takes time to learn. We have to be willing to work at developing these skills. Everyone admires the ability to stay firm, calm, and compassionate under attack, and everyone can develop it. Just remember that it doesn't come easily; it requires time and practice.

> When you are walking, walk.
> When you are sitting, sit.
> Don't wobble.

Everywhere, you can learn to focus your attention by doing one thing at a time.

We used to walk past an eating place called Chat and Chew. I never wanted to eat there. When I am chewing, I want to chew; when I am chatting, I want to chat. If I am enjoying something delicious, I don't want to discuss the weather, watch television, listen to music, or read the paper; I want to enjoy my meal. Even when I am having a cup of decaf, I prefer to enjoy my drink first and then give full attention to the conversation.

The Buddha said, "When you are walking, walk. When you are sitting, sit. Don't wobble." We need this advice today because we spend most of our time wobbling. We find it all but impossible to do just one thing at a time.

Years ago I went to see *Romeo and Juliet* presented by the Royal Shakespeare Company in San Francisco. I had been introduced to that play when I was about Romeo's age myself, in my little village school. I knew every important passage by heart and was deeply moved by the Royal Shakespeare presentation.

During the second act, I was thrilling to that paean to youthful love in which Romeo cries, "It is the east, and Juliet is the sun," when I heard a soft female voice rather unlike Juliet's implore, "Where's the candy, please?"

I didn't remember teaching that line in Shakespeare.

Then, with more urgency, the voice came again: "Where is the candy?"

I looked around and saw two high school girls. My grandmother, who could be blunt, would have told them, "You don't know how to enjoy a play, and you don't know how to enjoy candy either."

> Doing things with divided attention is just skimming the surface of life.

When we do things with only a part of the mind, we are just

skimming the surface of life. Nothing sinks in; nothing has real impact. It leads to an empty feeling inside. Unfortunately, it is this very emptiness that drives us to pack in even more, seeking desperately to fill the void in our hearts. What we need to do is just the opposite: to slow down and live completely in the present. Then every moment will be full.

A one-pointed mind makes beauty more beautiful. Music becomes more beautiful; painting becomes more beautiful; colors are more vivid and tones more dulcet. There is an inspired passage in Western mysticism where Thomas Traherne tells us that in his eyes the streets appeared to be paved with gold, and the boys and girls playing there looked like angels. "All appeared new," he says, "and strange at first, inexpressibly rare and delightful and beautiful." That is the intensification of vision, the seeing into the heart of life, which one-pointed attention brings.

> Whatever you are doing, give it your complete attention.

A one-pointed mind can be cultivated throughout the day by giving your complete attention to whatever you are doing.

While driving, for example, I suggest not talking to the other people in the car. I once rode with a driver who had probably never heard about undivided attention. We were speeding down the highway when he launched into a heated discussion, taking issue vigorously with something I had said the day before. Naturally, I wanted to explain to him why I thought he had misunderstood. But when he took both hands off the steering wheel to emphasize his point, I immediately exclaimed, "Never mind. Whatever you say. Just keep your hands on the wheel!" I still think it saved our lives.

On another occasion, when I was in Arizona to give a talk on meditation, I was enjoying a long ride through the desert with a friend when my eyes caught sight of a sign high up on a rock. It said, "You're supposed to be watching the road." Very helpful. While driving, our hands should be on the wheel and our eyes on the road – and so should our attention.

Most of us can understand the wisdom of this when it comes to driving, but it applies in life's less dangerous situations, too. In fact, it applies to the simplest of the routine activities that make up the day. In the kitchen, for example, the Buddha might say, "When you are cutting vegetables, cut vegetables." Talking and looking here and there only teaches the mind to wander. If somebody tries to get your attention, you can stop cutting and then give her your full attention. Many kitchen accidents can be avoided by this simple practice, but more than that, you are teaching your mind to make one-pointed attention a habit in everything you do.

Whatever job you are engaged in, I would say, concentrate on it completely. Give it your very best. That kind of focus will lift the burden from your shoulders, and you will find yourself doing much better work while enjoying it more.

Similarly, when the day is done, leave your work at the office. When we put a leash on our work and bring it home like a pet poodle yapping at our heels, we are neither here nor there, neither at work nor at home – which means we are not going to be at home anywhere. "Oh, this is not an ordinary dog," we say. "It's my pet. I have to take it wherever I go." But it is leading us instead.

I knew a professor like this. If a friend met him at the market and asked politely, "How are you today?" he would reply, "Oh, I have been comparing the metric patterns of Virgil and Homer." If you didn't run away fast enough, you would get a dissertation on Latin and Greek prosody right there next to the cheese counter. This is what I mean by bringing the poodle home: it's not just in your briefcase, but in your cranium too.

It takes a lot of control to work with concentration for eight hours and then drop your work at will, but this is one of the greatest skills that one-pointed attention can bring. When you enter your office, you give all your attention to your job; once you leave, you put the job out of your mind. This simple skill guards against tension and allows you to give your very best. If you have given your best, there is no need to worry about the results.

The amazing development of this habit of worrying is a significant comment on our times. I know people who put a great deal of effort into developing this habit. They practice it constantly. When they leave home, they worry about whether they have locked the door; they have got to go back and turn the key in the lock to make doubly sure. Then they realize they have left the key in the lock and have to go back a second time to collect it. They mail a letter and then worry about whether they remembered to write the address. If we lock the door and mail our letters with our attention on what we are doing, these little problems don't arise at all.

In fact, it is in these small matters of daily life that lack of concentration shows up easily. People worry because they don't concentrate. Here the Buddha uses a word I like very much: mindfulness. Whatever you are doing, he says, do it mindfully. Give it your full attention. We can guard ourselves against tension by learning to be mindful in everything we do.

The person who has control over his attention will always be mindful of what he is thinking, saying, and doing. Most of us, the Buddha implies, are not aware of these things at all. He compares our ordinary state of awareness to a dream: we are thinking, talking, and living in our sleep.

This is a compassionate way of describing the kind of fragmented lives we lead. It is because we are not really aware, the Buddha says, that we say and do unkind things. When we are fully here in the present, we won't say or do anything that is unkind.

> Through complete concentration, we
> can overcome the sense of separateness
> from the rest of life.

When concentration is deep, we may forget our body completely. In fact, we may forget altogether about that dreariest of subjects, ourselves. This is the real secret of happiness.

You may have noticed that when a lover of music is listening to a Beethoven sonata, you can tap her on the shoulder and she won't notice. All her awareness is on the music. Patanjali, an insightful teacher of meditation in ancient India, explains that this is the real reason for her enjoyment. Every ray of her attention is on the music, so there is no attention left for herself and her problems at all.

Albert Einstein had such a native genius for concentration that he often forgot himself completely. One of the most delightful examples of this is a story about Einstein at a dinner party with friends in Princeton. The after-dinner discussion went on and on into the small hours of the morning, until finally Einstein got up and said apologetically, "I hate to do this, but I must put you out now because I have got to be on campus tomorrow morning."

"Albert," his host said, "you are in my house."

This kind of absorption has its everyday difficulties, but it offers an extraordinary blessing. At a very deep level, people like this understand that the sense that you and I are separate, isolated creatures is no more than an illusion. Einstein called it "a kind of optical delusion of consciousness." To a great extent, he had lost any sense of being separate from the rest of creation. This awareness of unity is the distinguishing mark of spiritual awareness. Such people will consider you as part of themselves, and their welfare as part of your own. They will consider their "me" as part of "you." They will never think to harm you, because they are part of you; they will always think kindly of you, because you are part of them.

When attention is one-pointed, loyalty
will not waver; love will not wobble.

You can identify people with one-pointed attention because
they will be loyal in all their relationships. Those whose attention wanders easily are not capable of lasting loyalties. This is
one of the pervasive problems in society today, and the answer
is simple: to train our attention not to wander. When our
thoughts start to stray to fresh fields and pastures new, we can
call them back to stay in their own field, which makes that field
fresh and new every day.

The benefit of this simple skill is that when there are difficulties and differences in an intimate relationship, your loyalty
will not waver. Your love will not wobble at all.

There is so much friction and conflict in personal relationships today that disloyalty may seem inevitable. I have often
been asked by a man and a woman who were drifting apart,
"Have we lost our capacity to love? Is it not possible for us to
be loyal?" I don't reply to this as a moral issue; I present it as
an engineering issue. Without the precious ability to keep your
attention in the channel you choose, it is not possible to be
deeply in love or consistently loyal in your relationships.

It is because contemporary culture offers no way of training attention that we find good people, sensitive people, drifting apart. I have been able to help because I don't say, "You are
wrong; she is right. You are disloyal; she is loyal." I say, "You can
train your attention. You can teach it how not to wander." The

mind can be trained to such an extent that even if somebody
you love lets you down, you can treat that person with respect
and rebuild the relationship so that it is even more loving and
secure.

> You can change the channel of your
> mind from anger to compassion – just
> as you switch channels on your TV.

Life today is full of difficulties and conflicts. I think it was
Trotsky who said that anyone who wants to lead a peaceful life
has chosen the wrong time to be born. These are tempestuous
times, fraught with turmoil and violence – which means there
is all the more reason to have a well-trained mind.

When you have a mind that obeys you, you don't have to run
away when trouble threatens – and neither do you have to retal-
iate. You can receive opponents with respect and oppose them
resolutely, returning good will for ill will and love for hatred.
Very often, in my experience, this approach will sober an opponent enough that he responds to you with respect as well.

You train your mind to do this by switching your attention
just as you change the channel on your TV set. There are many
injurious channels in the mind, negative channels like anger,
greed, arrogance, fear, and malice. But for every negative emotion there is a positive emotion, and you can learn to change
channels.

I was at a friend's home when I learned to use a remote control to regulate the channels on his TV. My host said, "You just

point this thing at the television and change it to whatever you like."

Because you have been brought up in a scientific, technological culture – not always an advantage! – you see nothing miraculous about this. There may be no visible connection between the TV and the remote control, but it works, and you take for granted that there is a scientific explanation: the device sends a signal that allows me to change channels.

That is exactly what I do with my mind. When somebody is rude to me – which is seldom – don't think I am not aware of it. I am very much aware, but I can change the channel in my mind from anger to compassion as easily as changing channels on the TV. It's not good to let people walk all over us, and we may need to resist when they try. But we can resist without losing compassion and respect if we know how to keep our mind steady.

When your attention has been trained, if somebody does you a bad turn – which is very common in the world – you don't blow it up into something big. That is what attention does. When you give little discourtesies your attention, they get blown up into frightening proportions. If you don't give them attention, you simply brush them aside.

Similarly, little cravings that should not present much of a problem – an urge to eat this, smoke that, do this, say that – get blown up to gigantic crises. We feel we have to act on them or burst. These selfish urges are part of the human condition, but often all we have to do when they come is to turn our attention away. If we can do this, we can puncture even a big temptation and watch it shrink smaller and smaller and smaller while we get bigger and bigger and bigger. It's a strange, Alice-in-Wonderland world: where we saw a temptation towering over us and threatening to devour us, we find ourselves standing tall as a giant while a tiny temptation says, "Excuse me, may I leave now?"

> When we train attention, it will rest
> completely in the here and now, which
> brings limitless security and infinite joy.

Attention can be trained very naturally, with affection, just as you train a puppy. When something distracts your attention, you say "Come back" and bring your attention back again. With a lot of training, you can teach your mind to come running back to you when you call, just like a friendly pup. Don't try to be drastic with your mind. Don't act like a tyrant. Just keep patiently bringing attention back to the task at hand.

Friends of mine had a dog named Muka, of whom I was very fond. Muka was a playful creature with boundless energy, and whenever he saw something running, whether it was a rabbit or a truck, he had to run after it. But he was so devoted to me that whenever I called him, even if he had taken off down the road, he would come running back.

Our attention can be like that. When it sees a memory, it has to chase it, yapping, yapping, yapping at its heels. If it catches that memory, the memory has caught us. The moment attention takes off is the time to call, "Come back!"

After years of calling it back, the great day will arrive when attention will stay where we want it without our even needing to call. This is a glorious achievement, for it means there can be no resentment, no hostility, no guilt, no anxiety, no fear. Our attention will not dwell on any wisp from the past or the future. It will rest entirely here and now.

When our attention does not retreat to the past or wander into the future, we are delivered from time into the eternal now. To rest completely in the present like this brings limitless security and infinite joy. In the Upanishads, the perennial fountain of spiritual wisdom in India, the sages compute the joy of a person who has every material satisfaction the world can offer and say, "Let that be one measure of joy. One million times that is the joy of the person who rests completely on the present, for every moment is full of joy."

Ideas and Suggestions

Avoid doing two or more things at once, even if they seem trivial and you know you can manage it. If your job requires juggling many activities at once, try to give complete attention to one of them and take it to the next step before putting it on hold and switching to the next priority – which is what your brain has to do anyway. Practice being in control instead of driven.

When talking with someone, give that person your full attention, even if his attention wanders or she is saying something you dislike.

Remember the Buddha's words: "When you are walking, walk; when you are sitting, sit. Don't wobble."

When driving, give full attention to the road. Don't listen to music or talk to your passengers; explain that you need to concentrate. Similarly, when you're a passenger, don't distract the driver.

Don't bring your work home, in your briefcase or in your mind. And don't bring the problems of home into your work. Keep your mind here and now.

When your attention gets caught somewhere other than here and now – for example, in some past event you can't stop dwelling on – bring your mind back to the present.

Everything you do should be worthy of your full attention. If it seems worthy of only partial attention, ask yourself if it is really worth doing.

Remember that even if an activity seems trivial, when you give it one-pointed attention, you are training your mind.

CHAPTER 4

Finding Balance

*The energy we need is always
present; we just need to learn to
release and harness it.*

When I talk about a slower pace of life, I don't mean an idle sail far from any stirring breeze, with no adventure beckoning us. If anything is less desirable than a speeded-up life, it is a life of boredom and indifference. When we slow down and train attention at the same time, we are naturally cultivating enthusiasm for every day. We begin to face each task with energy and focus. This is a difficult balance to achieve – not hectic, not blasé – but it is a quality to be cultivated if we want to live at our best.

I found a good illustration of the challenge and rewards of this kind of balance when I went with friends to a favorite restaurant overlooking San Francisco Bay. We arrived early for lunch, so even though the place is very popular, we got a good table near the window. Soon I was completely absorbed in the scene. Outside the sun was bright and the wind was high.

Hundreds of seagulls were tossing about in the sky, and as many sailboats on the waves.

I couldn't help admiring the skill of some of the sailors. While we watched, one boat was racing toward us over the water with its sail almost dipping into the sea. My heart leapt into my mouth and I wanted to cry, "They're gone!" But the agile crew kept leaning out over the water on the opposite side, and the boat never quite turned over.

Others on the water were not so skillful. They would catch a strong wind in their sails and pick up impressive speed, but I would see their boats suddenly career erratically as if they had a life of their own. I could sympathize. How like life in today's restless, unpredictable world, where we often feel we are running before the wind in a stormy sea.

Below the restaurant window scores of other boats were tied up, hugging the shore, their lines slapping idly in the breeze. On their decks, men and women in summer clothes were enjoying drinks, chatting, or reclining in lounge chairs in the sun, perhaps dreaming that they, too, were sailors while their boats remained tied up comfortably at the dock.

Most of us have seasons like these sailors. At times we surge with energy, so much so that our lives are almost out of control. At other times we face blocks, can't seem to get on top of things, can't seem to move. Often these phases are accompanied by mood swings between high and low, ebbs and flows of self-esteem.

And, of course, there are times when we maneuver gracefully through events which at other times would have hopelessly becalmed or capsized us, navigating unerringly towards our goal. That is life.

According to yoga philosophy, the human personality is a constant interplay of these three elements – inertia, energy, and harmony. All three are always present, but one tends to be dominant at any given time – in a day, throughout a stage of life, over a life itself. And they lie on a continuum of energy. Just as matter can exist as a solid, a liquid, or a gas – ice, water, or steam – our own energy-states move in and out of inertia, activity, and harmony.

Inertia, of course, is least desirable. Energetic activity is much more desirable, but without control it only consumes our time and gets us into trouble. Harmony is the state we desire to live in. Fortunately, because all three are states of the same energy, each of these states can be changed into another. Just as ice can be thawed into water and water turned into steam, inertia and activity are both full of energy which can be converted into a state of dynamic balance full of vitality and power. That is what I meant when I compared Gandhi with a skilled driver behind the wheel of a Ferrari.

"It is not enough to be busy," Thoreau says.
"The question is, What are you busy about?"

It is wonderful to have abundant energy, for then no obstacle is too big to overcome. But there can be danger when a person has more energy than he or she knows what to do with. If we lack direction and an overriding goal, we are likely to misunderstand the signals that life sends us. Life is saying, "Come on! Venture out on the high seas, brave the adventures I send, and perfect the skills you need to fulfill your destiny." But we don't hear this message clearly. Somehow the signal gets garbled, and we can't tell where the call is coming from. So we pour our energy out into restless seeking, chasing fulfillment on Montgomery Street, with the bulls and bears at the stock exchange; or Union Street, with its fashionable boutiques; or Ghirardelli Square, where there seems to be a place to eat for every day of the year; or the night spots of North Beach. We can spend a lifetime like this and get nowhere.

Further, when we have a lot of energy we feel we have to act. We just cannot be idle. We get involved in activities and relationships primarily out of restlessness, and, because we cannot restrain ourselves even when we see the warning signs, we get into a lot of trouble.

Most of us know people like this. They have to keep going from morning till night, even doing things that are trivial. They have to keep busy, even if it means doing things that help no one including themselves. They simply cannot sit still.

"It is not enough to be busy," Thoreau pointed out. "The question is, What are you busy about?" This is a useful question. To know when to plunge into an activity and when to refrain from it requires judgment – detachment and discrimination. In India we have a saying, "Lack of discrimination is the greatest danger." When we lack discrimination, we do not know when to throw ourselves into something and when not to get entangled in it – and the more energy we have, the more it is going to get us involved in sticky, even dangerous situations from which it is difficult and painful to escape.

I think it is Henri Bergson, the French philosopher, who said that the human species should not be called *Homo sapiens,* "the creature that thinks," but *Homo faber,* "the creature that makes things." This is an astute observation. Most of us are concerned with making things: houses, roads, helicopters, guitars, pasta, anything. As long as we can make something, we find some satisfaction in living.

Take a walk in any large shopping mall and look in the shop windows. How many places are selling something that is necessary? How many are selling items that are beneficial? We can accommodate a whole mall in two or three shops if we rule out things which have been made just because *Homo faber* fever has got us.

Energy out of control has two
characteristics: hurry and worry.

Along the highway I used to see dusty Volkswagen buses with
their windows covered with stickers: "Paraguay," "Turista,"
"Mexico." We can tell the owners are travelers from the stickers they have collected – unless they just bought them in some
little shop at the mall. Similarly, if we observe a man or woman
who is the victim of over-abundant energy, we will see two
small identifying stickers: "Hurry" and "Worry."

Worry goes with hurry because people in a hurry don't have
time to think clearly and make clear decisions, so they are
always worried about results. They fret about the conclusions
of their research, about the value of their work, about whether
they are contributing to the welfare of their students. If you
slow down enough to think clearly and act wisely, you have no
need to worry because you know you are doing your best.

Energy, to be useful, has to be available
when we need it – at our beck and call.

One fascinating thing about people with a lot of energy is that
it's not at their beck and call. When energy is overflowing, it
tends to drive them; but at other times it dries up. This is the
other pole of our lives: the times when we just can't get going.

Often people have energy only when it comes to doing things they like. We all know people who have boundless motivation when it comes to doing what they want to do. They get absorbed in details that seem excruciating to us and pass hours without noticing how much time has gone by. But when it comes to activities that don't interest them, they may actually seem sluggish and even lacking in energy.

Most of us are like this. We have energy for activities that interest us, but when that energy is blocked it flows elsewhere, to something more attractive. We get busy doing those other, more attractive things and can't find time for what needs doing.

In India we call this "painting the bullock cart wheels." Just when the harvest is ready to be brought in, the farmer notices that the wheels of his bullock cart are looking rather shabby. Instead of going out into the fields, he takes a day to go into town for paint and then spends a week painting beautiful designs on the cart wheels. When he finally gets around to harvesting the rice, he has to work twelve hours a day just to keep up.

Even people who are usually energetic can have a mental block when a challenge comes to them. Students often grind to a halt on the eve of finals and find it physically impossible to open a book. I have seen students dismantling their motorcycles the night before exams, which calls for a lot more energy and application than the study of Wordsworth's "Ode to

Immortality." This is a valuable clue: the problem is not lack of energy, but how to control and direct it.

Most of us don't have to write papers on Wordsworth. But we do have to fill out our tax returns each year, turn in reports at work, write thank-you notes, clean out garages, and perform countless other tasks that we find distasteful. How many of us decide to put such things off while we work on our car or plant the new vegetable garden instead? Cars and gardens do need attention, but tax returns are urgent. In fact, when the calendar says April 14th, anything else is a distraction.

The energetic, restless, aggressive person is often looked upon as an achiever – a valuable asset who accomplishes much. People who are driven by their own energy can be like steamrollers, rolling relentlessly over any obstacle in their way. Yet when they face a task which promises no personal profit or power, the steamroller may become a rolling stone, perhaps even a sitting stone. Then it cannot push away obstacles; the most it can do is roll.

> Inertia is frozen power. The energy is
> there; it just needs to be released.

Just as water can freeze, thaw, and freeze again, our personal energy surges back and forth between activity and inertia. The energy is there, but it is sometimes frozen and sometimes out of control.

Look at what happens with most of us when we start a fitness program. We see some show on TV over the weekend and are filled with enthusiasm; we get expensive shoes and a fashionable outfit and go to bed Sunday night with the alarm set to go off early for a half-hour run before a good, nutritious breakfast. And for a week the schedule works perfectly. We have a keen appetite after the run, enjoy a nourishing breakfast, and feel invigorated for the rest of the day – all week long.

But when Saturday morning dawns and the alarm goes off, we're tired and sore. And after all, it is Saturday. There's no clock to punch at work. What does it matter if we have our run a little later? It's rather boring, and anyhow, rest is important too.

By the time we wake up an hour or two later, the sun is high and we remember we have a number of other things we need to do. There really isn't much time for a run. It's almost eleven when we get to breakfast. Since it's Saturday, we allow ourselves a sweet roll – with three cups of strong coffee to get going.

By afternoon, serious difficulties have set in. Someone has lent us an old paperback on UFOs, and it's just been lying around. It doesn't look particularly elevating, but we really should glance at it before we give it back. Remarkably, it proves rather gripping. After a few pages, we settle down on the couch and get into a comfortable reading position on our back. There is a package of cookies on the table, and we take one or two while we read. One or two won't hurt.

Eventually we realize that our hand is scraping the bottom of the bag. In fact, only one cookie remains. We're not particularly hungry any more, but we might as well eat it. We go on reading, and soon we have fallen asleep. We wake up just in time for dinner.

All in all, not such a good day for our fitness program. But it is better than the following day, when we can't seem to rouse ourselves out of bed at all.

We have a phrase for this in India: "a hero at the beginning." Plenty of energy at the start, but it fizzles out.

Or the energy cycle may start at the other pole. Years ago I saw an entertaining film about one of those rather seedy detectives whom you grow to love. The opening scene is still vivid. When the fellow drags himself out of bed in the morning he has a three-day growth of beard and can't even open his eyes. His movements are so sluggish that you think he must have been worked over by gangsters or be suffering from a serious hangover, but it turns out he's just a slow starter. He manages to get to the kitchen for a strong cup of coffee, and then discovers that he ran out a day or two before. Fortunately he hasn't done the dishes in a while. He finds some old grounds at the sink, pours in some boiling water, and drinks the result with a grimace while he lights a cigarette. We want to ask, "This is the hero? He can't even get himself dressed!" But then the phone rings, and the transformation begins. There's a crisis, someone's been killed, and within minutes this slow starter is a man of action.

Fortunately, there is a state beyond both phases of this cycle – beyond restless activity and sluggish inactivity too. The energy frozen as inertia can be released, and then all our energy brought under control in a dynamic balance that allows us to give our best and enjoy life to the fullest.

I appreciate the person who is energetic by nature, but I have special admiration when I see someone who suffers from lethargy learn to turn it into a torrent of activity. Vigor, vitality, energy, and will can all be developed. I have seen really lackadaisical men and women turn into dynamos. When they visit home again or go to a high school reunion, people say, "I can't believe it's you! You used to get up at ten and take an hour to eat breakfast. I've never seen you work so hard. What happened to you?"

Everyone likes a man or woman who has gusto and enthusiasm, but it is not enough to have an enthusiastic attitude and lapse when it comes to action. We need the energy and will to carry out our good intentions in whatever field of action we choose. Otherwise, even if we are enthusiastic, we won't be able to follow through; inertia will block our way. If we take to painting, we won't get beyond buying paints and canvas; if we decide to learn a language, we will get the books and tapes but not find time for Lesson 2.

> Having all our energy in a dynamic
> balance allows us to give our best and
> enjoy life to the fullest.

Inertia is like driving with your brakes on. A surprising number of people do this; their brakes are set all the time.

Once, when Christine and I were driving along next to the university – where, fortunately, the speed limit was twenty-five miles per hour – we began to smell something like burning rubber. Christine was distressed, but the car seemed to be functioning all right and we were almost home. It was only when we reached our house that we discovered the emergency brake had been on the whole time. I didn't know it was even possible to drive that way.

That is just what happens when we are in a state of inertia. We may have gas in the tank and an engine in top condition, but no amount of potential power helps if we drive when the brakes are on. On the other hand, it means there is no irremediable problem. All that is required is to release the brake.

When energy surges, we have the opposite problem: no brakes at all. Then we can't stop. We have to move, have to act, have to get involved – which means we can get caught in virtually any activity under the sun.

Often – though not always! – what we get caught in is something we enjoy. Once we get caught in it, however, we can't think about anything else. I have known many people who tell me that they think about their work day and night because they really enjoy what they do. But they can't turn it off. They can't keep from taking their work home or working late at the office, and they can't turn off their minds when it's time to sleep. When you talk to them, they are not really listening to you but thinking about their work or their hobby. They may not realize it, but what once seemed so pleasant to think about has become a burden.

We can get caught in anything: in fashions, in collecting things, in shopping, in furniture, in yard sales. We can easily get caught in cars and food and computers. These are the things that drain our energy and our time. And once we get caught, we begin to get speeded up, trying to keep up with where our hobby leads us. One friend confided in me that he had got caught like this in taping old movies on TV. After a while he was spending hours at it, sitting through late shows so he could avoid taping the commercials. He realized things were out of hand only when he caught himself staying up until two in the morning to tape a movie he didn't want so that he could trade it to someone in his video club. And don't you know people who complain that they have so many plants that they haven't time for anything but watering and cutting and spraying?

I'm not at all saying there is anything wrong with video

collections or houseplants. But there are times to cultivate the garden inside: time to reflect on what we are doing, what we value, how we are spending our lives. *Homo faber*, "the maker," has to stop incessantly making and doing in order to become *Homo sapiens* – truly wise.

We need time for pondering life's deeper questions instead of always making money or making things. We need time simply to be quiet now and then. There is an inner stillness which is healing, which makes us more sensitive and gives us an opportunity to see life whole.

> We need time simply to be quiet now and then: time to reflect on what we are doing, what we value, how we are spending our lives.

To live in balance, we need to drive the way skilled highway patrol officers do: ready to accelerate if necessary, but always ready to brake when the situation starts to get out of control.

Do you remember those dual-control cars in which you learned to drive? Picture the will – your capacity for discriminating judgment – sitting in a dual-control car as the driving instructor, and desire as the student at the wheel. As long as Desire is driving correctly, Will doesn't need to do a thing. But the moment Desire starts to do something dangerous, Will takes the wheel, touches the brake, and says, "That's no way to drive."

Desire retorts, "How do you know what I was going to do?"

"By the look in your eye," Will replies.

When Will is in control, he can tell from the gleam in the eyes of Desire that what is about to happen is not going to be good for your health, your nerves, or your sleep.

Of course, in the early days, Desire is going to thump on the steering wheel and howl and say, "I'll call the highway patrol!"

But Will just replies patiently, "I am the highway patrol."

After a while Desire comes to know that Will is his friend. Thereafter, if there is any difference of opinion, instead of looking upon Will as somebody hostile, Desire will say, "Will, this is something I can't handle." And Will says, "Leave it to me."

This is a perfect picture of the state of balance. It is not that you lose your desires, but your will is always in control. Wherever desire is in control and the will lags behind, there is likely to be trouble – emotional distress, psychosomatic and physical ailments, personal entanglements with painful consequences. These are the problems of energy running out of control. But when will and desire are in harmony, you enter into a state of perfect driving – with power steering, power brakes, power everything. This is victorious living.

Living in balance means living in the
present, ready for whatever comes.

As a boy, when I discovered Charles Dickens, I was so
enthralled by his stories that as I neared the end, I would read
only a couple of pages at a time to make the pleasure last. My
little niece was like that with chocolate; when she got a bar of
Cadbury's, she would take just one lick and then wrap it up
again and put it aside.

This is all right for children, but when our mind treats life like
a bar of chocolate, it will be looking for chocolate all the time. It
will always be restless, which is the root cause of all our hurry.
And, of course, a restless mind can't ever be at peace – and how
can we expect a mind that's not at peace to find joy anywhere?

When you live in balance, you are in joy always – not joy in
the sense that things always take place in the way you want, but
because you are never disturbed and have a quiet confidence
in yourself that cannot be shaken. It is one of the fallacies in
our modern approach to life that we believe we can be happy
only when everything takes place exactly as we want. Actually, I would say that it's a good thing life doesn't work that way.
Sometimes the best things in life are not what we thought we
wanted at all, and the unpleasant experiences are what helped
us grow. When your life is in balance, you lose the capacity to
be disappointed.

Once I took Meera and a few other friends to see Agatha Christie's *The Mousetrap*. Meera is an Agatha Christie fiend, so she had been looking forward to this outing for some time. When we arrived, however, we found a crowd of disappointed people standing near the box office bemoaning the fact that the theater was already full.

In my earlier days I would have been crushed by this kind of catastrophe. My mind would have protested, "I've been looking forward to seeing *The Mousetrap*, and now there's no room even for mice!"

But today, mainly as a benefit of the practice of meditation, I have lost the capacity to be disappointed. My thoughts were on my niece, looking bravely devastated beside me.

We had to make a decision right on the spot. I got a paper and discovered that there was one show in a theater near us that we could reach in time – a movie starring Woody Allen, whom I don't profess to understand.

Meera and our friends perked up, though, so I said, "Let's go see Woody Allen." The only scene I could relate to in the whole movie was when Woody Allen introduces the same question that the Hindu and Buddhist scriptures ask: "How can we ever enjoy anything in life when we know that we have got to die?"

"Oh," I said, "this is going to be a great film." Then it took off in another direction, where I couldn't follow. But Meera and the others enjoyed themselves thoroughly, so I did too.

When your life is in balance, you lose
the capacity to be disappointed.

When harmony predominates, it means your mind is at peace,
so you cannot be disappointed. It also means you become an
utter stranger to loneliness. When you are with people, naturally you are at one with them, but the incomprehensible thing
is that when you are alone, too, you are at one with the world.

I enjoy being with people. It is not social enjoyment; it is not
even intellectual enjoyment. It's a kind of enlightened rapture
of being one . . . always. In the early days, I used to feel at home
only in a small circle who enjoyed the things I enjoyed. Today
I relate to everybody. When I go out, I like to sit in a corner
somewhere and just watch "me" passing in many disguises.

I can't tell you the joy of this. I can be in any country on the
face of the earth, I can be with any people, and I will always feel
deeply, "These are my people." Then you are a good friend to
your friends and a good friend to those who are not so friendly
also. When people praise you, you are at peace; when they criti-
cize you, you are still at peace. You are not any better because of
the praise and no worse because of the censure.

This kind of peace of mind cannot be disturbed by any external circumstance. With it you live in freedom, which is the real
fruit of slowing down.

Ideas and Suggestions

It is important not to confuse slowness with lethargy. In slowing down, attend meticulously to details. Give your very best even to the smallest undertaking.

When it is difficult to start a project or task, try to take the first small step towards completion. For example, if you resist writing a thank-you note to your aunt, tell yourself that you will just get out the stationery and a pen. Often, once this small step is taken, the job will be completed quickly.

When you feel driven to act on an impulse, take your time to ask if this is really what is in your best interest.

Observe the ebbs and flows of energy in your day. When are you most alert and energetic? What drains your energy? With careful observation you will be able to identify the swings of energy: perhaps too much caffeine or sugar has left you agitated, and then exhausted. When we see these swings more clearly, we can take steps to enrich our performance, patience, and inner peace.

Most of us find we have energy for jobs and activities we enjoy. Try doing with enthusiasm a necessary job that you don't particularly enjoy. Put the task you dislike first on your list. With training, you can actually begin to juggle these likes and dislikes to release more energy into your life.

If your life seems cluttered, ask yourself if you have got caught in some hobby that may be harmless but time-consuming. Are you spending more time than you'd like on a pet hobby, a cherished collection? Even worthwhile activities can come to dominate our time if we do not consciously ask this question now and then.

CHAPTER 5

Living in Freedom

*To live in balance we need a
mind that listens to us, not one
that drags us about as it
pleases.*

To enjoy anything, we cannot be attached to it.
William Blake understood this beautifully:

> He who binds to himself a Joy,
> Doth the winged life destroy;
> But he who kisses the Joy as it flies
> Lives in Eternity's sunrise.

What we usually try to do is to capture any joy that comes our way before it can escape. We have our butterfly net and go after the joy like a hunter stalking his prey. We hide and wait, pounce on it, catch it, and take it home to put on our wall. When our friends come to visit, we say, "Hey, Stu, would you like to see my joy?" There it is on the wall – dead.

We try to cling to pleasure, but all we succeed in doing is making ourselves frustrated because, whatever it promises, pleasure simply cannot last. But if I am willing to kiss the joy as it flies, I say, "Yes, this moment is beautiful. I won't grab it. I'll let it go." And I live with a mind at peace and a heart untroubled.

Pleasure comes and it goes. When it goes, we don't need to cling to memories of past happiness or dwell on when it may come again. When we turn to the past in yearning, we are running away from the present. When we propel ourselves into the future in anticipation, we are running away from the present. This is the secret of what the world's spiritual traditions call detachment: if we don't cling to past or future, we live entirely here and now, in "Eternity's sunrise."

> Likes and dislikes don't have to be rigid.
> We can learn to play with them, and the
> freedom can be quite enjoyable.

When I get an opportunity to do something enjoyable – to attend a good play, an interesting movie, a fast soccer match, or game of tennis – I do enjoy it. But I don't let my mind dwell on the event before it happens, and if something requires me to drop my personal plans, I can do so without any lingering disappointment. That is a wonderful development, and it comes through training the mind not to have rigid likes and dislikes.

Often, rigid likes and dislikes are merely a matter of attention getting stuck. We get caught in a groove of what we have been conditioned to like or dislike, and we can't imagine getting free. When we find that others have their attention stuck in their groove too, friction results.

Usually, without thinking, we react negatively and move away. But we can learn to play with our likes and dislikes instead, and once we taste the freedom this brings, it can be quite enjoyable.

Suppose you and your partner are trying to decide what to do on Saturday night. You have been reading reviews of a new film, but she wants to see a local production of *As You Like It* – even though she knows Shakespeare bores you silly. You have been looking forward to your movie; she has been looking forward to her play. What are you to do?

When Saturday arrives, you might say firmly, "I'm going to see my movie." She will say just as firmly, "Fine, then; I'm going to see my play." If you are caught in these rigid choices, you are not only not going to spend Saturday night together, you will gradually find you spend less and less time together doing anything. You get used to doing what you want, and if you are rigid in one thing, you are going to be rigid everywhere else. Rigidity is a habit of mind, and if left to its own it will grow more and more unyielding.

If you want to free yourself from being dictated to by your own habits like this, you can turn your attention away from your film and accompany her to *As You Like It* instead. You'll miss your movie, but you will gain her appreciation.

You don't like Shakespeare. You don't like blank verse. You

detest ballads. But you go, and you give the play your complete attention too. I have seen people dragged to the theater to please their partner; they can't pay attention, so they sit through three acts thinking about something else. Of course, they have a miserable time. But that's not what you do. You give all your attention to the play, trying to follow the language, and after a while your interest gets caught – perhaps by those glorious words:

> All the world's a stage,
> And all the men and women merely players.
> They have their exits and their entrances,
> And one man in his time plays many parts,
> His acts being seven ages. . . .

"Hey," you say, "this is rather good."

You have never been able to pay attention to Shakespeare, and now you're getting interested – just because you wanted to move closer to a lover of Shakespeare. At the end of the play you admit, "You know, I really enjoyed myself. Honestly!" And you *are* being honest: you enjoyed it through her eyes.

Training the mind to be patient begins
with wearing likes and dislikes casually,
like a favorite old sweater.

It is not possible for a mind that is rigidly conditioned to slow down because such a mind is in constant turmoil – roiled like the surface of a lake in a high wind. What gives power to the wind is what I call "likes and dislikes." To put it simply, the mind is conditioned to go after what it likes and to avoid what it dislikes, and so it is never at rest.

If we can observe our mind with a little detachment, we can watch this process. I've done this countless times. When faced with some trifling dislike – perhaps a dinner that is not to our taste – it is natural for the mind to experience a slight downturn. Similarly, when we get the dessert that we like, the mind puts on a smile. There isn't much danger here unless such likes and dislikes become rigid – but if they do, they can wreak havoc with our peace of mind.

Training the mind to be patient and calm under all circumstances, then, often begins with learning to wear our likes and dislikes loosely, casually, like a favorite old sweater.

There are many other benefits of this. If we can become less rigid in things like films and food, we will be freer in other areas too. We will find it easier to face a task at work that we don't like but must be done. At times when things don't go as planned, we will be less likely to get frustrated and disappointed. And, most important, we can work with people we don't like without our peace of mind getting rumpled.

Please understand that I am talking here about personal preferences, not about questions of value. We make legitimate, important distinctions every day – for example, between real

food and junk food or between healthy and unhealthy lifestyles
– which are not a matter of what we like or dislike. Problems
arise because it is easy to confuse likes and dislikes with what is
right or wrong.

Unfortunately, what we like is easily confused with what is
best for everyone. The difference is really between what is pleasant and what is of lasting benefit. Pleasure is fleeting; a real benefit lasts. Sometimes, it is true, they coincide. What is pleasant
can be beneficial. But usually this is only with something simple, such as a glass of orange juice. Most of the time, we need
to scrutinize the credentials of any experience that promises to
please us and ask: "What are the long-term effects of this experience? What are the costs – not just in dollars but in calories,
security, relationships, or self-esteem?"

I have always enjoyed movies, for example, but it is more and
more difficult to find something I want to see. A good film is
hard to uncover among the hundreds that are filled with exces-
sive, graphic displays of violence. It is not merely that I do not
enjoy movies like this; I don't approve of what they do to my
mind.

Once again, the Buddha had a very practical touchstone for
questions like these. In his eyes, everything we do shapes the
kind of person we are becoming. So he says, "If an experience
calms your mind, slows you down, makes you more likely to be
compassionate and kind, that experience is beneficial; you can

enjoy it. If it agitates your mind, speeds you up, excites your senses, or makes you angry or resentful, it is not beneficial; you should avoid it."

> With every choice, take time to ask, "What are the long-term effects of this experience? What are the costs – in calories, security, self-esteem?"

Likes and dislikes come in the way of love. A rigid person may expect others to enjoy what he or she enjoys. But people have ideas of their own, and other people often enjoy things that leave us cold. To love, we have to learn to loosen our own personal preferences and expectations. Then we can enjoy, if not the things they enjoy, at least their enjoyment of those things.

A friend once confided in me, "I find it extremely difficult to talk with my father, and it saddens me because I want to get closer to him. We don't argue or anything; we just care about such different things. When he starts to talk about golf, I want to scream. I have no interest in golf whatsoever. Of course," he added, "I would never tell him that."

"Then it's simple," I said. "You don't need to have any interest in golf. What you're interested in is your father. Just listen to him and not to the golf."

This is not just for parents and children. It is in little ways like these that companionship grows and the benefits of each other's experience are shared. After all, trying to make other people fit our likes and dislikes is likely only to make us move farther apart. If we care about a relationship, instead of always trying to force the other person to come our way, we can look for opportunities to go his or her way, which is good for both.

> By observing how the mind responds
> to food, you can get a precious early
> warning when your mind is starting
> to get out of control.

Food is an excellent arena for learning to juggle with rigid likes and dislikes. Most people are nutrition-conscious today. We are aware that there is a difference between what is good for the body and what merely appeals to our taste. But we still get swayed by old conditioning when it comes to certain favorite foods.

I have seen children turn their faces away and say "Icky, icky, icky" when they are served something they don't like. But we older people are not so different. We may not say anything out loud, but inside we too turn away and say "Icky, icky, icky" when life presents us with something we don't like.

I can sympathize with this easily. Today I am free of likes and dislikes where food is concerned, but that freedom was won only after a struggle. As a boy, like most Indians, I could not imagine enjoying a meal without hot chilies and spices. It was through Gandhi's example that I began to understand that this isn't a healthy diet. Immediately, I began to reduce spices and salt.

For some time afterward, I confess, my meals didn't taste very good. In fact, they seemed not to have any taste at all. But today, after many years of training, I am free. I can taste my food now instead of tasting only the spices in it, and if I were served a meal of highly spiced, deep-fried food, I wouldn't find it enjoyable at all.

By juggling with my likes and dislikes this way, I have changed my eating habits completely. Today one of my great favorites is asparagus, which I had never heard of in India. Today I consume such quantities of asparagus that the checkout clerks can't believe the amount I buy.

You might be surprised to find the topic of food in a discussion about patience and peace of mind, but taste is one of the sure barometers of inward weather. When I was suffering through a winter in Minneapolis, there was a big sign over a bank that would say "Sunshine" or (much more often) "Snow" or "Storms Ahead." It's like that with the palate. When your mind is under control, your taste buds will ask politely for food that is good for you. But when you are speeded up, your palate is likely to clamor for its old favorites – and you are going to be much more vulnerable to its demands. In this way, by observing how the mind responds to food, you can get a precious early warning when your mind is starting to get speeded up or out of control.

This connection between food and the mind is unsuspected today, when people are subject to trifling likes and dislikes every day. There seems to be no end to the division and subdivision of taste. When I want ice cream I have one hundred and forty-seven varieties to choose from, and it's not enough to want chocolate; I have to decide between possibilities like Dutch, Bittersweet, Super Fudge Wonder, and Chewy White Chocolate Macadamia. (Often I just tell the clerk, "Give me the one you like best.") And for coffee I have to specify Sumatran, Colombian, Kona, or one of a dozen other varieties. I know people whose whole day is affected when they can't get the coffee they like made just the way they like it. As our preferences get fractioned finer and finer like this, the range of what we can tolerate narrows to a slit – in everything, because this is a habit of the mind.

I used to go with friends to a nearby coffee shop before my evening talk. One person would order coffee with low-fat milk; a second had to have it with half-and-half. A third took her coffee black and a fourth only drank decaf. I myself am partial to espresso decaf – and one of us insisted on tea.

One evening I suggested, "Why not let one person order the

same for everyone?" That is what my mother used to do. At tea time she would make a big pot of tea the way she liked it, with whole milk fresh from our cow and a little sugar, and serve it to everyone. We all enjoyed it, and it never occurred to us that we should have a special beverage made to our personal specifications.

> Preferences can get more and more rigid
> until nothing is right, nothing will please.

We have all known older people who find it impossible to tolerate any change of scene or routine. They must sit in the same chair, watch the same programs on TV, eat the same dinner, have the same conversations over and over again. Anything new would not fit into their rigid scheme. And they explain, "We're too old to change."

If left alone, preferences like these get tighter and tighter until finally nothing is comfortable; nothing will please. The room will always be too cold or too hot, the food too rich or too plain. The neighbor's dog will be too loud and your friends will not speak loudly enough. Nothing will be quite right.

But it is not only older people who get caught like this. I had a friend who found it disturbing to eat in restaurants – not because he didn't enjoy the food, but because they never arranged the service the right way. As soon as he sat down, he had to rearrange everything: the knife, the fork, the spoon, the glass, the napkin. If a salad fork was not provided, he would ask for one, even if he did not order salad. And he would always order a second spoon – I'm not sure for what. He would be visibly nervous until everything was just so. The arrangements, in fact, were much more important to him than the food, which I would have thought to be the first priority while eating in a restaurant.

This kind of rigid behavior is harmless, however difficult it may be to live with. But consider the person who simply must have things his way or lose control completely. I see items in the papers where a fight breaks out because one person is too slow at a green light or takes another person's parking place. Most people would just shrug when this kind of thing happens. Some feel forced to use strong language. But what of the man who pulls out a gun and shoots another man dead over a parking place? Has rigidity gone so far that he simply can't tolerate any violation of what he wants?

> We can learn not to be rigid by playing
> with likes and dislikes in little things.

Such incidents are still rare, though I am afraid they are becoming more common in our hurried world. But on a smaller scale,

115

this kind of thing goes on all the time. I often see people get upset over a minor deviation from routine.

When I was teaching on my old campus in India, I used the blackboard often. The physics department had the best blackboards, so I got permission to use their hall when it was not occupied, and they suffered me to teach Shakespeare and Milton where only Newton and Einstein could be mentioned before.

Now, I am right-handed, so I always kept my chalk on the right side of the board. And every day I would go in expecting the chalk to be there and find it at the other end of the board instead. Patiently, I would pick it up and put it where it belonged. But I did get a little irritated. I would ask myself, "Why can't these physics people leave their chalk in the proper place?" And at the end of my class I would place it again to the right.

This little drama happened every day, to the great entertainment of the students. If they came in and found the chalk left inadvertently somewhere else, they would considerately move it to the wrong end of the board.

Then one day it occurred to me that the physics professor who played the other role in this drama must be doing the very same thing: finding that I had left the chalk at the wrong place for him and having to move it every day before starting his class. Perhaps he wasn't even right-handed.

That afternoon, when my class was over, I carefully placed the chalk where he would keep it.

I did this for a couple of days and nothing happened. I thought all was well. Then one day I came in and found the chalk on the right! Instead of leaving it where he wanted it, he was placing it where it would be convenient for *me*. It was a marvelous illustration of how ready we are to assume that our way is the only way – and how, if we only go the other person's way a little, he might move in our direction too.

> Training the senses does not mean
> depriving them. It means educating
> them – teaching them not to demand
> things at our expense.

We can have rigid likes and dislikes about anything from clothes to opinions, but the most practical place to start loosening them is with the senses: our little preferences in what we taste, smell, watch, listen to, and touch. Freedom from the tyranny of likes and dislikes begins with training our senses to want what we approve of and to obey when our judgment says no.

Training the senses does not mean denying them or depriving them. It means educating them not to demand things that will cost us in health, security, or freedom. In training the senses, we don't forfeit anything in life of lasting value.

Sight, hearing, taste, touch, and smell are the channels that connect the mind to the outside world, and the study of the interaction of senses and mind is most fascinating. Just as the body assimilates food, the mind assimilates what the senses take in. In yoga psychology, in fact, it is said that we eat through our senses. What we experience becomes part of who we are.

Most of us are careful about the food we eat, but in terms of what our senses eat, we exercise little judgment at all. We forget that we are eating constantly, especially – whether we are reading a book, watching a movie, or listening to music – through our eyes and ears.

The senses should act as the mind's office staff, the mind's assistants. The mind is the boss, at least in name. But all too often the boss doesn't boss, and the senses behave like boisterous companions trying to get the mind to have a good time. "Hey," the eyes say, "take a look at this new red sports car. Isn't it terrific?"

The ears say, "Studio quality audio – just listen to the sound!"

Touch says, "See how soft the upholstery is!"

Smell says, "Don't you just love that new car fragrance?"

Taste, for once, is at a loss, but he finally steps forward and says, "Great! Let's get in and go get some pizza."

Often all these five characters talk at once. In fact, very often they don't even agree; they are trying to get the mind to pay attention to different things altogether. That is what happens if we eat a good meal and watch a movie at the same time. No wonder we feel confused! And with all this ruckus, who has a chance to hear the still, small voice within?

To enjoy life in freedom, we have to train the senses to listen to us, for the simple reason that attention follows the senses. To do this, it is not necessary to deprive ourselves of good food or good entertainment, but simply to enjoy what is beneficial and ignore indulgences we will regret afterwards.

When the senses are trained, they are alert and sensitive. There is a sense of freshness and newness about everything. Instead of feeling you are in the same old groove, you find choices to be made all the time.

In other words, the kind of life I am talking about is not a life bleached of color. It is just the opposite. I don't think I have ever known anyone who enjoys life more fully than I do, ups and downs alike. Everything that is good, everything that is wholesome, everything that is beautiful can be enjoyed. What is important is that we not cling to it, but enjoy it as part of a life that is lived for a goal higher than our own personal pleasure.

> Permanent joy is far, far higher than
> pleasure that comes and goes.

One of the main difficulties in grasping this is that we don't have anything lofty to compare with the humdrum pleasures of sensory experience. Until we have tasted something higher and longer lasting, it's hard to understand what spiritual figures in all ages keep trying to tell us: "Permanent joy is far, far higher than pleasure that comes and goes."

Unfortunately, permanent joy isn't part of our lives, while passing pleasure is something we are used to – a dependable feature of our human state. When some sensory experience promises to please us, we cannot think of anything else or imagine there could be anything higher. We get into a fever of longing until we get whatever it is that we want. Only then does it turn out to be not so important after all. I remember a line from James Thurber that captures this perfectly, something about "peach ice cream not tasting as peachy as it used to."

It is human nature to go after passing sensory gratification. We want it, and want it, and want it ... until we get it. Then we are likely to find that it isn't as peachy as it used to be, and it is already gone. Yet we always think the next time it will be peachier.

At the outset, when something pleasant comes our way, we say to ourselves, "What could be more satisfying than this? What could be sweeter?" We do not know that in the long run this sweetness can turn bitter. What is beneficial, on the other hand, may be bitter at the outset – a fitness program, for example, or a low-fat diet. But after a while, as we begin to enjoy the benefits, we see that what seemed bitter is truly sweet, for it brings the happiness we wanted all along.

In San Francisco, when Christine and I had business to do in one of those massive old office buildings from the thirties, I was introduced to another marvel of American technology: the revolving door. This particular building had a big, heavy glass door that carried a lot of momentum, and once I got in I couldn't get out. Every time I neared an opening, the door would slap up behind me and push me past; and the harder I pushed to get around to try again, the faster I was pushed around. I thought I was going to be trapped there permanently. That is the feeling: you just can't stop; you have to keep going round and round.

Seeing I was in trouble, Christine called out, "All you have to do is stop."

I stopped, the door stopped, and I was free.

That is what happens when the senses get out of control. The revolving door keeps hitting us from behind – slap, slap, slap, slap! – and we keep running faster and faster, not realizing that the faster we go, the more we will be urged to go even faster. In order to get out of the trap, we have to slow down the thinking process so as to get control of it, then begin to change our likes and dislikes so we can get free.

I think it is Oscar Wilde who says, "I can resist everything except temptation." When a friend is yielding to a sensory craving that is going to harm him, it is easy for us to see how easily he could overcome it. "Jonathan," we say, "why don't you just

step out of the revolving door? Turn your back on the temptation. Just say no." Only when such things happen to *us* do we
experience how difficult it is to go against a conditioned craving. We need to allow ourselves a wide margin for mistakes
while learning to resist old, rigid habits – and to allow our parents, our partner, our children, our friends, and even our enemies an even wider margin for the mistakes they make, too.

I am talking here about what G. K. Chesterton called "tremendous trifles." It is my experience that most of our temptations don't come in titanic proportions; usually they are little,
little trifles. There is some drama in fighting a great temptation, where the whole world is watching as if its fate depended
upon whether we win or lose. The real challenge is to resist
puny cravings that nibble at us like mice. While we are looking toward the left, one mouse takes a nibble from the right;
when we turn to the right, we feel a nibble on our left. We can't
even take these nibbles seriously – until we find that we've had
a third helping of dessert or an extra drink for the road. Life
consists of trifles, Chesterton says, and how we deal with them
is the substance of our lives.

Remembering how quickly time passes
adds meaning to every moment.

The Buddha called life a sea because the sea is moving

constantly. All the world's great religions remind us that we are sailing on an ocean of impermanence. Every experience is transient. Even this body, with which we identify ourselves, changes from day to day. This body of mine is not the same as it was last year. And what about the mind? In the language of Buddhism, the mind is a process, changing all the time. It is a succession of desires. If we satisfy one desire, another will follow; if we satisfy that, a third will come. No experience can bring permanent satisfaction because there is a limitless series of desires, one behind another, in the vast sea of consciousness.

In this world of change, the Buddha reminds us, time is passing very, very quickly. It is not a negative reminder. To remember this truth does not take away from the joy of life; it adds meaning to every moment.

Some time ago Christine and I took a group of children to Ghirardelli Square in San Francisco. It was summer and the city was crowded with tourists, so it took a long time even to find a place to park. For a moment I even wondered if we should have gone elsewhere. But I had only to look at the children. To them the crowd was part of the attraction, and they could hardly wait to get out of the car and join in.

We wandered through Ghirardelli for a while just looking into the shops, enjoying the mimes and jugglers, and counting the different languages we heard around us. Distractions and color and noise and confusion reigned. The children were in heaven. While they explored the sights, Christine and I found a bench a little to the side and from there simply watched the crowd.

Eventually we joined the long line in front of the old Ghirardelli Chocolate Factory, which we found crowded with pilgrims in search of the perfect chocolate. If it's available anywhere in the world, it must be available in Ghirardelli Square, and people from as far away as Munich and Tokyo were there to enjoy it. I was watching the crowd and looking around to see what was the great favorite of the day. Almost everyone was paying their respects to the hot fudge sundae, so we ordered hot fudge sundaes for the children too. Christine and I shared ours with one of the youngest – which meant that we didn't get the cherry, we didn't get the chocolate, we got only spoonfuls of what ice cream was left melted in the bowl. We didn't mind; we were there to enjoy the enjoyment of the children.

At several tables, I saw people actually photographing their chocolate confections. This was something I had never seen. They were like patrons in front of a painting at the museum, or like pilgrims at a temple; there was the same worshipful glow in their eyes. The person with the camera would direct people as if he were on a Hollywood set, trying to get everything just right, from the arrangement of the napkins to the big red cherry on top. But the curious part was that after the pictures had been taken, they were too speeded-up to pay much attention to their sundaes. They kept talking about the next attraction: Golden Gate Park, Pier 39, the ferry ride on the bay.

I'm sure we sat at our table much longer than anyone else, but the management didn't seem to mind. We did not want to hurry. We felt no need to rush to be anywhere else. We had everything we wanted right there.

Ideas and Suggestions

When you find yourself daydreaming – for example, anticipating some special event – bring your full attention back to the present. When the event arrives, focus on it completely. If you find yourself dwelling on it afterwards, bring your mind back to the present again. You're teaching your mind to enjoy without grasping – and to be present here and now.

Go on a leisurely outing with family or friends, doing what they like, enjoying their enjoyment.

To practice patience, listen to a friend with concentration even if you find the topic boring.

Observe your day to see if media exposure is adding to your impatience or diminishing your peace of mind. One way to bring more peace into your life is to avoid agitating movies, programs, and music.

Time for Relationships

We all need personal relationships if we want to function beautifully in life's ups and downs.

Years ago, when automation was still new to me, I went to San Francisco with a friend. On the way, she stopped at her bank for cash. "It will take only a minute," she assured me.

I thought this unlikely, especially because we didn't even enter the bank but joined a queue in front. There was a machine there but nobody to take care of her transaction. Curious, I approached the man in front of us to watch what he was doing.

My friend got an apprehensive look on her face and whispered hurriedly, "Let's not stand so close. He's using his secret code, and he won't want us to see it."

That was my first encounter with automatic tellers. I must say it was convenient to get the transaction done in two or three minutes. But I couldn't help but feel sorry that this was one more small incident where technology has replaced the human presence, where being in a hurry has eliminated any time for human interaction. Even the sparse human contact that used to exist between teller and customer has been broken.

Whether it is the little exchanges between a bank teller and a customer or the fundamental relationships that shape our lives – our ties to partner, parents, children, friends, and co-workers – human bonds are becoming more and more tenuous in today's world. Partly this is because we simply do not take time for human companionship. Personal relationships cannot be left to chance, especially in a speeded-up world. But even in the midst of distractions and stress, we can learn to shape our relationships if we are willing to take the time to do so.

If we have been slowing down the pace of our life, practicing one-pointed attention, and loosening our likes and dislikes, we should begin to see the benefit of these new patterns in all our relationships. For these are some of the tools that can help us make for ourselves a personal world rich in companionship.

> The real essentials of life – compassion, kindness, good will, forgiveness – are what is fundamental to living as a true human being.

In order to re-create a world of personal connections, it is important first to understand just how impersonal the lives of most people have become. We are used to hearing "mod-

ern progress" affirmed categorically. It is helpful to remember that although we have made important advances in certain
fields, we have regressed in other areas that are essential to our
humanity. Where certain crucial human virtues are concerned,
we lag far behind our ancestors.

Autotellers, telephones, fax machines, and computers are
unquestionably useful, but they are not fundamental. The real
essentials of life are compassion, kindness, good will, and for-
giveness. It is qualities like these that are fundamental to living
as a true human being – and that is where our age lacks a great
deal.

There is a place for mechanization; there is even a place for
automation. But our modern way of life touts mechanization
for the sake of the machine and automation for the sake of automation, and everything for the sake of speed. I see everywhere
the rapid advance of these forces that strike at our humanity,
corrode our sympathy, and make us almost like machines ourselves in a world of machines.

> Relationships can be beautiful –
> if we take time to nourish them.

I am in a special position to illustrate both sides – the human
versus the mechanized, the loving versus the hurried – because
I come from a world where life was rich in personal relation-

ships, from the richest person to the poorest, the most educated to the most illiterate.

I am not idealizing India. India has many problems. But
there is a bright side too, and part of it is this richness of personal relationships.

I grew up supported by intimate relationships. In my ancestral family, which is matrilineal, the day-to-day influences on
my early life came from the women, and particularly, of course,
from my grandmother and mother. The three of us were always
together. I spent every day with them and never grew tired of
their company.

When I was in high school we had an hour's break for lunch,
and the school was about a mile away from my home. Many
students used to bring their lunch, but not me; I had to have
my meal with my granny and my mother. As soon as the bell
rang I would run all the way along the paths through the rice
fields, working up a big appetite. When I reached home my
lunch would be ready, timed perfectly. My granny would sit on
one side and my mother would sit on the other, and there was
nowhere else in the world I would rather have been. Nothing
was allowed to interfere with this time spent with my family.

It was the same story in the evening. I always wanted to go
right home after my soccer game because I knew my granny and
my mother would be waiting for me, wanting to hear all about
my school day and the game. I related every detail because they

were interested in everything. Every friend of mine at school was known to them by name; every play I had made on the soccer field was replayed for them.

This is how my grandmother and my mother laid the foundations of security in my heart. I knew that I came first with them, every day, always, and it gave me a confidence that has withstood every storm life has brought me.

It is not that my grandmother spoiled me. She was a terribly tough teacher. I was not allowed to get away with anything. But she would always stand by me. She pointed out my faults, which were many, and she never connived at what I was doing if she disapproved. Yet under no circumstances would she undermine my faith in myself. This kind of spiritual teaching is a great art, and she was a master of it.

When I was ready to leave for college, she didn't try to dictate my career or influence my course of studies. In India it is common for older people to give strong advice to younger people, and several of my uncles told me in no uncertain language that I should pursue a course in engineering. My grandmother told me simply, "Follow your own star." She didn't try to tie me to her. She said, "All your mother and I want is that you go out into the world and make us proud that we gave birth to you."

I know that circumstances today in our modern way of life are very different from those that surrounded me as a boy in my village. Yet some things are universal. I believe that our relationships with our children, like all our relationships, can be beautiful, though it takes a lot of time and patience. This is what my mother and my grandmother taught me by their way of life.

This simple truth is ignored in our speeded-up world. While appreciating the technological advantages of our modern civilization, let us take time for relationships and cultivate – and help our children to cultivate – the timeless values and fundamental virtues that make us human.

> It is through personal relationships that we learn to function beautifully in life throughout its ups and downs.

We all need the little human contacts of life, and we all need intimate personal relationships with family or friends. I am aware that many people today do not live with a family, but that is not the issue. Whether we live alone, with family, or with friends, we can cultivate daily personal relationships. This is precisely where our modern way of life fails us, because it deprives us of the time and the opportunities we need to sustain these relationships.

We can cultivate personal relationships everywhere, in everything, every day. I like to have a relationship with each person in my life, even the bank teller and the mail carrier. When I first took up residence in Berkeley, I developed a

CHAPTER SIX   133

friendship with the postman. In those days – it seems hard to believe if you don't remember – mail was delivered twice a day. I used to get many letters from family and friends, and after a while their delivery became a personal affair. "Hey," the carrier would say, "there's a letter for you from India today!"

I would tell him, "That's from my mother," or "That's from Meera's mother," or "That's from one of my students." He learned all about my family and told me all about his. Soon we had a personal bond. He was not just delivering letters; he was bringing me messages as a friend.

On those special occasions when I would receive a package, I would say, "Wait a minute, and I'll show you what this is." I'd open the package and even share the contents with him if it happened to contain something I could share.

We can reverse the tendency of our civilization to impersonalize everything by making an effort every day to see other people as people, not objects. I'm sometimes asked, "What does it matter whether you have personal relationships at the bank? It's simply a business transaction, and the quicker it can be conducted, the better." But these transactions do not have to be impersonal. When I was still new to this country I went to a small bank where I could get to know the people who worked there. I was interested in them, so they became interested in me. After a while, when I entered, it was not as an anonymous customer. I would greet them with a smile and they would ask me what news I had from home. I used to spend a few minutes chatting with the people there and got to know them rather well.

Things didn't begin that way. On my first day there I made out a check in the Indian style, writing the word "Self" where it says "Pay to the order of." The teller had never seen a check like that, and she turned to the others as if I didn't exist and said, "This guy doesn't know how to write a check."

I laughed along with everyone else. Then she came to hand me the money and gave me quite a bit more than I was entitled to. I said to her, "This is a good bank. Here is a customer who doesn't know how to write a check and a teller who doesn't know how to count the money!" She laughed, a little embarrassed, and after that we were friends.

All this banter makes for relaxation. Even now, despite the convenience, I never deal with autotellers. I like to talk to a human being. These are not just financial transactions. They are human relationships in which trust and concern for each other can grow.

Such personal ways do take time, of course. When you know a transaction is going to take a little longer, you simply plan accordingly. The appeal of the autoteller is that we don't have to plan; we can get money at the last minute – assuming the machine is open and is not malfunctioning. Is that gain worth even a small loss to our humanity? Is anything worth the deprivation of human relationships?

> Trust, intimacy, and concern can
> flourish when there is personal contact.

Everywhere today I see fewer and fewer personal contacts between people, which means fewer and fewer relationships where trust, intimacy, and concern can flourish.

Television, for example, apart from its other drawbacks, has had a devastating effect on human companionship. We say we do not have time to talk to our neighbors, let alone the teller at the bank or the mail carrier; yet the surveys consistently show that we watch, on the average, five or more hours of television every day.

When people say to me, "We don't have time for all this," I ask, "How many hours a day do you watch television?"

They count and say sheepishly, "Oh, about four."

I just suggest, "Why don't you cut it in half?"

I do not ask people to eliminate television, but why not keep it within reason? I do watch good shows on television, though they are few and far between. But even then I like to watch with friends. We enjoy each other's company, and we are together not just physically but in spirit too.

Nothing makes us feel so secure as
knowing that we have brought a little
joy into the life of someone we care
about.

Most of us want to be liked by those around us. We like to please
and be loved by those we love. And nothing makes us feel so
secure as knowing that we have brought a little joy into the life
of someone we care about. As John Donne said, "No man is
an island." That is why selfless relationships lead to happiness,
while a self-centered life leads to loneliness and alienation. As
human beings, it is our nature to be part of a whole, to live in a
context where personal relationships are supportive and close.

Yet although it is natural, this is one of the first things to be
forgotten when we get speeded up. Because when the mind is
going too fast, it is impossible to be sensitive to the needs of
others. It is impossible to resist the insistent little voice inside
that demands, "You have got to get your way!" So often, this is
what damages loving relationships in our hectic world.

I was fortunate as a boy because I had a loving grandmother
who taught me not to insist on always having my own way. In
my early years, of course, I tried to test my will against hers.
Don't think I didn't try quite a few times! Sometimes it worked
with my mother, too. But never with my granny – not even
once.

In India, one of the easiest ways to bring mothers and grand-mothers to their knees is not to eat. Children learn this at an early age. You just say "Don't want!" and your mother gives in, your granny gives in, and you get your way. I had seen quite a few of my cousins doing this, so I said to myself, "Why don't I try it too?"

One morning at breakfast, I tried it on my mother. She was really shaken. "I made it specially for you," she coaxed. "Just taste it. Once you taste it, you will like it."

In fact, she had prepared especially beautiful rice cakes that morning, and the coconut chutney was most tantalizing. There was nothing I wanted more than to eat that breakfast. Except one thing: I wanted to get my way, too.

So I stubbornly pushed my plate away.

My granny came in at that moment, just returned from the temple, and she saw immediately what was going on.

She sat down next to me and began to comment on the breakfast. "These rice cakes are as light as a flower. And look at the special chutney from fresh coconut. Your mother has made it all for you. Don't you want to eat it?"

Again I pushed my plate away.

"All right," she said, "then I'm going to eat it myself."

"Why don't you, Granny?" I said, not thinking she would.

She just sat there and ate it all. Not one bite was left! I had learned an important lesson: never to trifle with my granny.

My mother was always softhearted. After a while she said, "I can make fresh rice cakes for you."

My granny said, "He doesn't want to eat them." I still wanted to get my way. I couldn't bring myself to say, "All right, I'll eat them up." I stuck to my self-will and went without my breakfast.

My granny must have done this three or four times, and after that I never bargained about food – never in the kitchen, never at mealtime. That strategy was left out; there was never any confrontation over food. And my grandmother would explain to my mother, "You see, you have to do that with children. That is the way they learn." My mother understood, but she retained her soft heart. She was not like my grandmother. I was fortunate to have both these wonderful women to raise me: my grandmother, who I realized years later was my spiritual teacher, and my mother, who I came to think of as her teaching assistant.

All children try at times to get their way like this and bend their parents to their will. My mother always said that I was an angel until I went away to college; but my granny, while she respected me deeply and in many ways had much higher ambitions for me than I could ever have had for myself, knew that I was far from perfect. In her tough but tender way, she taught me over and over to turn my back on my self-will, because she knew that I would be crippled in all my relationships if I carried that habit into my adult years.

Later on, when I was a teenager, if she had to tell me not to do something, she felt that since I was past childhood she should give me a reason. I would just say, "You don't have to tell me the reason, Granny. I won't do it." She used to brag to the entire village, "Is there any other boy in this village who will say he doesn't want to hear the reason?"

This is the kind of perfect relationship that comes as the stubbornness of self-will subsides. When you don't always insist on your own way, love, trust, and respect come naturally. The greatest relationship can exist between older people and younger people when they share this kind of trust.

> When irritations or conflicts occur
> in a relationship, don't move away.
> Move closer – even if it's hard.

We expect professional and financial success to require time and effort. Why do we take success in our relationships for granted? Why should we expect harmony to come naturally just because we are in love?

Naturally there are going to be differences when two people are in love. Even identical twins have differences of opinion, and they come from the same combinations of genes and the very same background. Why should two people from, say, New York City and Paris, Texas, expect life together to be smooth sailing?

When irritations or conflicts occur in a relationship, my advice is, don't move away. Don't say, "I am not going to talk to you; I don't want to see you." Instead, that is the time to say, "I am going to get closer to you anyway. I am going to try to put your welfare first."

There is a very close connection between patience, kindness, and love. Yet this word "kindness" is so simple – so humble perhaps – that we seem to have forgotten what it means. It opens a great avenue of love. Most of us can be kind under certain circumstances – at the right time, with the right people, in a certain place. If we find ourselves unable to be kind, we may simply stay away. We avoid someone, change jobs, leave home. But in life we often have to move closer to difficult people instead of moving away.

I believe that it comes naturally to us to want to contribute to the welfare of those we love. But I am enough of a realist to understand that there are obstacles that stand in the way of the free flow of concern and compassion for those around us. If we understand these obstacles, we will be better prepared to overcome them.

In most disagreements, it is really not ideological differences that divide people. It is often self-will, lack of respect, putting ourselves first instead of the other person. Sometimes all that is required is listening with respect and attention to the other person's point of view.

Instead, most of us carry around a pair of earplugs, and the minute somebody says something we don't like, we stuff our ears until we can start talking again. Watch yourself the next time you find you are quarreling with someone you love. It won't look like a melodrama. It will be more like a situation comedy on television: two people trying to reach an understanding by not listening to each other. One person is saying, "What did you do the other day when I asked you to wash the dishes?" And the other replies, "What about you?" Can you imagine anything more ridiculous? They are not trying to settle their differences; they are trying to make sure that neither of them will forget.

To stop this quarrel, simply listen calmly with complete attention, even if you don't like what the other person is saying. Try it and see. Often the action will be like that of a play. For a while there is the "rising action": his temper keeps going higher, her language becomes more heated; everything is heading for a climax. But often enough, the ending is a surprise. The other person begins to quiet down. His voice becomes gentler, her language kinder – all because you have not retaliated or lost your respect. Whatever happens, you walk away feeling better about yourself. You have stayed kind, kept your cool, not let anger push you around. The taste of freedom that brings is worth any amount of practice.

> The more defenses we carry, the more
> insecure we feel – because defenses
> prevent us from moving closer to others.

In personal relationships, most of us are far from free. We are always wondering how the other person is going to react – always fearing an attack, a snub, or perhaps just indifference. So we have all kinds of ego-defenses – moats of suspicion, drawbridges of diffidence, walls of rigidity, and several inexplicable trapdoors. With all of these barriers, we expect to sit in our citadel undisturbed, the ruling monarch of our realm. But just the opposite is true. In fact, the more defenses we have, the more insecure we feel, because it is these defenses that prevent us from moving closer to others.

When we practice giving our best without getting caught up in others' attitudes and reactions, we find that they often begin to lower their defenses, too. Little by little, centimeter by centimeter, the walls begin to come down. Then they too can give their best to the relationship without anxiety or fear.

If just one person in a group is always on guard, it is natural for everyone else to raise their defenses also. It becomes a reflex. As soon as we see someone who is on guard, we say, "He makes me feel uncomfortable." We retreat into our citadel, draw up the bridge, close the trapdoors, and wait until he goes away. But the secure person, the person who is comfortable with herself and tries to remember the needs of others, makes everyone else comfortable as well.

> To love, we need to be sensitive to those around us – not racing through life engrossed in all the things we need to do.

So much of the richness of life is to be found in companionship that I cannot stress strongly enough how important it is to heal bonds that have weakened and to bring freshness back to relationships that have grown stale.

Most relationships begin to fall apart through disagreements, and disagreements are not settled by argumentation and logic. They are resolved – or, more accurately, dissolved – through patience. Without patience you start retaliating, and the other person gets more upset and retaliates too. Instead of retaliating with a curt reply, slow down and refrain from answering immediately. As soon as you can manage it, try a smile and a sympathetic word.

There is a close connection between speed and impatience. Impatience is simply being in a hurry. Our culture has become so speeded up today that no one has time to be patient.

People in a hurry cannot be patient – so people in a hurry cannot really love. To love, we need to be sensitive to those around us, which is impossible if we are racing through life engrossed in all the things we need to do before sunset. In fact, I would go to the extent of saying that a person who is always late will find it difficult to love; he will be in too much of a hurry. A late riser will find it difficult to love; she will always be going through the day trying to catch up.

> Anger can be contagious – but so can peace of mind. Which do you want to spread?

It takes some self-knowledge to understand that when we associate with people, we participate in their mental states. We are affected not just by what people say and do, but also by what they think.

When we are thinking angry thoughts about somebody, we are throwing abstract rocks at him. Sometimes I think a rock does not hurt so much as a harsh thought, because the hurt from a rock can heal much more rapidly. We know how long people can suffer because of resentment and hostility.

Living in a place where people are angry and impatient is living in an atmosphere worse than smog. We are all concerned about pollution of the atmosphere we breathe, but internal pollution is equally dangerous. One angry, impatient person can upset a whole group.

Conversely, have you ever known anyone whose mind was so calm that agitated people find rest in her presence and angry people become forgiving? People with the skill of putting others first often play this role. Without preaching to others or advising them, the peace of mind they radiate has a transforming influence on those around them.

We all need support, whether in a family context or in the context of companionship among friends. And I believe we can find it, even in our hectic world.

The Buddha might have called this "right companionship." Everything we do, he reminds us, either adds or subtracts from our own image as human beings. We can seek out the goodness in people. We can seek out what is noble in human character. We can look for goodness and nobility in choosing our friends, in choosing to whom to give our attention and our love.

We cannot afford to give unquestioning admiration to a person simply because he or she happens to be prominent in the media. Everywhere we look – television, newspapers, magazines, books – such individuals are played up. They are not meant to be role models; they are simply gifted athletes, musicians, actors, or actresses. But because of the constant attention of the media and our innate need to have someone to look up to, they take on an aura of supreme importance.

Rather than looking to the media for love and inspiration, isn't it better to look around us? If we confuse media glamour with reality, we are going to find it very difficult to love. Whether we realize it or not, we will always be expecting perfection, which means we will be increasingly disappointed, frustrated, and insecure.

> There is only one way to be completely happy: to forget ourselves in the service of others.

In my early days of teaching in San Francisco, someone in my audience once asked, "You are an educated, cultured, enlightened person. Do you believe in hell? Do you believe in heaven?"

"I have seen people in hell," I replied. "And I have seen one or two people in heaven, too."

If you look back upon your own life – at the times when you were filled with anger, when your mind was in turmoil, when you couldn't sleep – you have been a visitor to hell. But in those rare moments of self-forgetfulness that come to all of us, when you forget your petty, personal desires in helping your family or community or country, you pay a brief visit to heaven right here on earth.

Gandhi, in whose India I grew up, lived in heaven always.

He was a citizen not just of India but of heaven too. When the people of India were blessed with good fortune, which was seldom, he was immensely happy. But while they were suffering under the burdens of poverty, famine, and the injustices of foreign rule, he lived in heaven because he was able to help relieve their suffering by showing them how to stand on their own feet and resist injustice nonviolently. Heaven and hell are just two states of mind.

My grandmother used to say in her simple language that there are millions of people who suffer because they make demands on life that life cannot fulfill. Even after centuries of civilization, we still haven't discovered that there is only one way to be completely happy, and that is to forget ourselves in the service of others. When we forget ourselves in trying to add to the welfare of others, happiness comes to us without our asking.

When you look around in any country, you are likely to find a few men and women who have this remarkable gift of being able to forget themselves. These are the people who live in heaven. All their attention is on others, so they don't have attention left over for dwelling on what they want and insisting on their own way. They don't have time to keep asking, "Am I happy? Is the world tending to my needs?" They are occupied only in giving, only in loving.

To live in heaven always, we have to slow down the mind. All negative thoughts are fast. They are going a hundred miles per hour, so of course we can't turn, we can't stop, we have got to crash. But positive thoughts are slow. Patience is always in the slow lane. Good will is never in a rush. And love is actually off the highway, for it is not a stream of thoughts at all but a lasting state of mind.

If you could see into the minds of people in a hurry, you would see thoughts whirling round and round like the laundry in a dryer, faster and faster. Such people get angry without any convincing reason – over trifles, over little pinpricks that would be laughable if the consequences weren't often disastrous – all because the mind is racing out of control. And there are physical implications, as I said earlier. When the mind is going too fast, it naturally begins to affect the body, because body and mind are not separate; they work together.

> It is love that is important – the harmony
> of your home, the harmony of your
> workplace, the harmony of your life.

That is why I say, be patient with your partner, your co-workers, and your friends. Give plenty of time to your children. If they take up valuable time narrating some after-school adventure, what does it matter? If your partner forgets to inform you that she will be coming home late from work, or is late in picking you up at the airport, your mind needn't race out of control. It is love that is more important – the harmony of the home, the harmony of the workplace, the harmony of your life.

Everywhere, take your time, so that you do not give the mind an opportunity to speed up and get out of control. When you keep going faster and faster, you can't even be aware that your mind is racing or that you are being insensitive to the needs of others.

Do you remember the scene in *My Fair Lady* when Eliza accuses Professor Higgins of being insensitive? He reacts with utter amazement. "Insensitive?" he replies. "Me? I am the soul of sensitiveness. Consideration is my middle name. Kindness and I are never parted." This is the self-image most of us have: "I couldn't possibly be selfish or insensitive or unkind." And, in a sense, it is true. Most of us are not unkind people; the problem is the racing, speeded-up mind. To be sensitive, we have to place the highest priority on slowing down and giving full attention to what we do and to everyone we live and work with.

As the mind slows down from sixty thoughts per minute to fifty, to forty, to thirty, to twenty, we begin to see people more and more clearly. Even in many intimate relationships, people don't really see each other. That is why they act insensitively: they hurt each other, not willfully, but because they simply don't see. In order to see those around us, to understand their needs and reflect on how we can contribute to their welfare, we need to slow down the furious activity of the mind.

Learning to love comes easily when we remember the needs of the whole. We simply have to ask: What will benefit my family most? What will benefit our children most? What will help us to make a contribution to life? If we ask these questions, we shall find we are learning to love naturally – and that our welfare, too, is included in the welfare of the whole.

Ideas and Suggestions

Cultivate personal relationships in all your activities. It will help to reverse the depersonalization of our world.

Dwelling on yourself builds a wall between you and others. When you find yourself dwelling on your own needs, your own wants, your own plans, your own ideas, turn your attention to the needs of others.

When you find you are getting impatient and want to get your own way in some little matter of convenience, try putting the other person's comfort and convenience first. You can begin within the circle of your family and friends, where there is already a basis of love and respect on which to build.

Make a game of finding ways to remember the needs of the other person: let him choose dinner for both of you, for example, or go to the film she wants to see.

Share activities with your children. Enjoy their enjoyment.

Don't compete in any relationship. Look for ways to complete each other instead.

When differences arise, remember that to disagree, it is not necessary to be disagreeable.

Take time to listen with complete attention and respect – there may be less to disagree about than you think.

Share your times of entertainment with others. Relaxation is an important part of learning to slow down.

CHAPTER 7

A Higher Image

Body and mind are like a car
that carries us through life. But
they shouldn't be driving us
– we are the driver.

It is said that Arthur Schopenhauer, the German philosopher, was walking about one night plunged in thought when a policeman, naturally suspicious, approached and asked him, "May I know who you are?" Schopenhauer paused for a long time before he replied, "I wish I could tell you."

This is the central dilemma of our civilization: we are born, go to school, get jobs, get married, have children, grow old, and pass away without ever knowing who we are. And the question we should ask is: "If I don't know who I am, what is the use of anything I do? If I don't know who is doing it, if I don't know who is enjoying life, what earthly use is it?" That is why the Upanishads say that the joy that comes when we discover who we are is a million times greater than all the pleasures the most advanced material civilization could offer.

Every problem we have today, from stress and difficulties in personal relationships to the devastation we are causing to our environment, can be traced to this fundamental lack of understanding of who we are. For this is what is at the root of our lack of a higher purpose. As long as we believe that we are physical creatures – which is what the mass media are dinning into our ears day in and day out – we cannot help trying to satisfy all our needs in physical ways.

As long as I look upon myself as no more than physical, I have an incomplete idea of who I am. This inadequacy is even more fraught with danger than in earlier times because the media reinforce it every day. Almost every movie we see, every book we read, every advertiser we listen to says, "You are incomplete; you will always be incomplete." And then they offer us some ephemeral object or transitory experience that promises to satisfy us temporarily. Only rarely does someone arise to remind us that we are not incomplete but whole – not imperfect physical creatures, but essentially spiritual beings whose greatest need is simply to discover our real nature.

"All that we are," the Buddha says, "is the result of what we have thought." Our health is to a great measure the result of what we think of ourselves. Our environment is the outcome of what we think we need as human beings. Virtually every aspect of our lives is directly affected by the image we have of the human being. And today, to put it simply, we look upon ourselves as the body. We try to satisfy ourselves by satisfying the body, and the more acute our inner hunger grows, the more desperately we seek. It never occurs to us that the body is only a house and we are the tenants – or, to use a different metaphor, that the body is a kind of car and we are the driver.

The manager of the bank in a small town near us once told me that if people don't see his car in the front of the bank, they think he isn't there. On the following day they ask him, "Why didn't you come in yesterday?" They identify him with his car.

This happens to me, too. My wife and I used to walk regularly at a nearby beach that is privately owned. In the early days, the teenagers who check the passes never recognized us; they recognized our car. As long as we were in our own car they would wave us through, but if we came in a friend's car, we would have to show our pass. I wanted to tell them, "Please look inside. It's not the car that has the pass. We have the pass. We're not our car."

Today it is different. Once we got to know them, they stopped looking at the car. Instead they look at us, smile, and say, "Enjoy your walk!"

In the same way, when our relationships become personal, we don't identify people by the body they happen to drive. We get to know the person inside.

Unfortunately, if we think of ourselves as physical, we may never get even a glimpse of the person inside. We will see only the outer image. To me it has always been a matter of grief that even an intelligent person may not see parents or partner, children or friends, after living with them for years.

> We are not imperfect physical
> creatures. Our essence is spiritual, and
> our greatest need is simply to discover
> our real nature.

Many people would agree intellectually that the human being is more than physical. But if you look at the way we live – at work, at play, in the shopping center, at home, in the theater, on the playground – you will see what our real self-image is. We don't have a high image of the human being. In fact, we have such a low image that books often become best-sellers by telling us what a low type we are. Countless movies and plays become popular by reaffirming this idea that we are no more than physical, only slightly removed from our evolutionary forebears in the animal kingdom.

We are so set in this belief that I find it difficult to convince people of anything else. If I say, "You are an exalted creature, with a spark of the divine within you that nothing you do can extinguish; and you have been granted life in order to give, because it is in giving that we receive," they find it hard to believe. Today, amidst all this conditioning to the contrary, we need constant reminders of our higher nature, and that is why

I recommend spiritual reading as one of the points in my Eight Point Program.

There is no more absorbing reading than the great mystics and scriptures of the world's spiritual traditions, which offer a vast selection from which to choose. We needn't limit ourselves to just one tradition, either. Every religious tradition has inspiring literature, and by reading widely we see that, as one of India's most ancient scriptures puts it, "Truth is one, though we call it by many names."

My advice is to set aside a particular time every day, perhaps fifteen minutes to half an hour, to read from an uplifting book of spiritual instruction or inspiration. First thing in the morning and last thing at night are both very good times. Even a short period of quiet inspiration in the morning will anchor the rest of your day; and at night, particularly after a hectic day, there can be no better preparation for sleep.

The events of the day follow us into our dreams, and when we watch television at night or read agitating material, we carry those images and that agitation with us into our sleep along with the rest of our problems. Millions of people read popular fiction at night to get their mind off whatever is agitating them, but these stories only add to the images left over from the day. The techniques presented in this chapter offer a much more effective way to fall asleep with a calm mind, so that we sleep refreshed and awake with spirit renewed.

A short period of quiet inspiration in
the morning will anchor the rest of
your day.

We are so physically oriented that only seldom do we glimpse
the pulsating world within us – the world of thoughts, feelings,
urges, and desires. This is a world unto itself, a world that never
sleeps, never rests. It is the world of the mind.

Physically, at least, we are able to rest a little every night. But
mentally we are seldom at rest. The body sleeps but the mind
never. This has enormous practical consequences, for a great
deal of our vital energy is consumed by the mind. The faster the
mind races, the more gas it consumes. When we wake up feeling that we do not have enough vitality, enough drive, enough
joy of living to make it through the day, we are probably victims
of an energy shortage. This happens to millions of us because
we don't know how to minimize the continuing energy con-
sumption of the mind – not only while we are awake, but while
we sleep as well.

The most practical and immediate tool we can use to slow
down the mind is what in India is called a mantram or mantra: a name or phrase with spiritual meaning and power. All
the world's great spiritual traditions recommend this practice,
though of course by different names: in the West, for example, it is sometimes called "the prayer word." The mantram has

immense power to slow down the speed of the mind and lift its attention from any problem that is troubling us. At the same time, it helps to fill our consciousness with a higher image of who we are. The mantram is a living symbol of the profoundest reality we can conceive of, the highest power we can aspire to and love. When we use a mantram, we remind ourselves of our true nature and hold before our mind's eye this highest image of ourselves.

The mantram is an effective brake on the speed of the mind. When the mind is racing in anger, anxiety, worry, or greed, we can use the mantram to slow it down – a skill that is every bit as essential for secure living as good brakes are for safe driving.

In India we had an official called the brake inspector, who was authorized to stop any car on the road and demand to see how well the brakes worked. If you did not prove to him that you could stop your car in a reasonable distance, you would have to have your brakes repaired.

With the mind, too, we need some kind of inner inspector to see whether there is any brake on our anger. Usually he will be forced to say, "You don't have any brakes at all! How do you manage to drive?" Then he will give a citation, because a mind without a brake is a source of danger to us and to those around us too.

If you have power brakes, when you encounter a danger-ous situation while driving you have only to touch the pedal to stop the car. Similarly, when your mind is beginning to race – beginning to get angry, to get afraid, to get greedy – you are entering a danger zone where you need some kind of power brake to get your mind under control. That is what the mantram can do.

Repetition of a mantram is a dynamic discipline that gives access to inner reserves of strength and peace of mind. Every one of us has these deep inner reserves; we simply do not know how to tap them. The mantram gives us a way to regain our natural energy, confidence, and balance.

> The mantram has immense power to free
> attention and flood our consciousness
> with a higher image of who we are.

There are two basic tools for mastering the thinking process. One is repetition of the mantram; the other is meditation. Half an hour of meditation every morning slows down the thinking process. Then, during the day, the mantram keeps the mind from speeding up again.

It is important to distinguish these two. As I teach it, meditation involves sustained concentration on the words of a scripture or great mystic. No matter what one's religious affiliation, the Prayer of Saint Francis of Assisi is a perfect example:

Lord, make me an instrument of thy peace.

Where there is hatred, let me sow love;

Where there is injury, pardon;

Where there is doubt, faith;

Where there is despair, hope;

Where there is darkness, light;

Where there is sadness, joy.

O divine master, grant that I may not so much seek

To be consoled as to console,

To be understood as to understand,

To be loved as to love;

For it is in giving that we receive;

It is in pardoning that we are pardoned;

It is in dying to self that we are born to eternal life.

By contrast, the mantram is not a passage, but a word or short phrase with spiritual meaning and power. The mantram can be repeated anywhere at any time, while meditation requires a quiet place and a set period of time. And the mantram can be used by anyone, while meditation requires discipline and dedication.

In short, these two complement each other beautifully in several ways, as you will discover yourself when you try them.

I have great sympathy with people who find it hard to meditate. It *is* hard. In the Indian scriptures, taming the restless mind
is compared with trying to tame the wind. Nevertheless, I know
of nothing on earth that can remotely compare with the benefit
that even a little practice of this powerful discipline brings.

Over the years, I have learned a great deal about how to present meditation so that it can have maximum benefit in our
modern way of life. My instructions are based on my personal
experience and addressed to people who have tasted what life
has to offer and long for something more. Meditation is the
basis of a life of splendid health, untiring energy, unfailing
love, and abiding wisdom. It is the very foundation of that deep
inner peace for which every one of us longs. No human being
can ever find lasting satisfaction in money or success or pres-
tige or anything else the world can offer. What we are really
searching for is not something that satisfies us temporarily, but
a permanent state of joy.

This word *meditation* is used today in many different ways.
The method I teach is the one I have followed in my own life,
which I have presented to thousands of Americans over the
years. It has two important aspects. First, it slows down the
mind, making it increasingly calm, steady, and clear. It does
this by sustained attention on a single focus: the words of an
inspiring passage that embodies a lofty ideal.

The second aspect is less obvious: since we are what we

think, we become what we meditate on. The sustained attention we give to our meditation passage drives it deep into our consciousness, so that the ideals it embodies gradually become part of our character and conduct.

Obviously, it is important to choose such passages with care. They must be positive, practical, universal, and inspiring. They should reflect authentic spiritual experience. And they should present the highest possible image of the human being.

All the passages I recommend for meditation are chosen from the world's great religious traditions, and they are universal as well. They embody the conviction that God is to be found within us and a spark of the divine is present in every human heart.

Because this conviction is found in every major spiritual tradition, using passages from different sources is like looking at Mount Everest from many different perspectives. You get one view of the Himalayas from India, another from China, a third from Pakistan, a fourth from Bangladesh, a fifth from Tibet. But these towering peaks are always the same, like the power that is present in each of us as our real Self.

I learned to meditate in the midst of an extremely busy life at a large university in India, where I had many cultural interests and responsibilities from early morning until late at night. That is why, when somebody comes up after one of my talks to say, "I would like to learn to meditate, but I don't have time,"

I don't take it too seriously. I know from personal experience that everyone can find half an hour a day, especially for something so rewarding.

> Meditation on inspired words drives them deep into consciousness. The ideals they embody gradually become part of our character and conduct.

Meditation is a demanding discipline, but it pays rich dividends. Today, after years of practice, my attention is effortlessly one-pointed all the time. Whatever I am doing, it is like driving smoothly on a highway without ever having to change lanes.

I may not have a California driver's license, but I am a fully licensed driver of my mind. I wish you could see me driving the car of my mind – just cruising along. Most of the time I can put my feet up and just roll along on cruise control. You won't see any weaving; you won't see any speeding. I just drive in one lane. And as long as the mind is traveling in the same lane, anger cannot come, fear cannot come, greed cannot come. For all of these negative states, the mind has to change lanes.

There is a marvelous skill in this that you will develop with practice. Once you have learned this skill, instead of getting agitated and afraid when old memories come, rattling their chains and wearing ghoulish makeup to frighten you, you can sit back and say, "Good show! Are you quite through?" The ghosts of the past will have no hold whatever on your attention, which means there is no emotional connection at all.

My observation, after many years of meditation, is that most problems are much smaller than we think. It is by dwelling on them, brooding on them, feeding them with our attention, that we make them bigger and bigger. When we learn to direct our attention to something positive, the problem often shrinks to its proper size, making it much easier to deal with –and much less intimidating, too.

> The promise of meditation is simple:
> we discover who we are.

Even if your mind wanders thirty times in thirty minutes of meditation, if you keep bringing it back to the passage, you have done wonderfully. You may feel you have wasted your time, but that discipline will go on paying off throughout the day. Over the months, as the bank advertisements put it, it all adds up. Eventually, you may be bringing your mind back only ten times. Then it will be only once or twice. Finally, if you practice systematically and with sustained enthusiasm, the day has to come when you do not have to bring the mind back even once because your attention never wavers.

I cannot describe to you the splendor of this experience. All your attention is completely integrated, focused like a laser on the words of the passage. Your senses close down and you are blissfully unaware of your body. In this supreme experience you know that the body is not you, but only the house in which you live. You feel a presence stirring in the depths of your consciousness, so healing, so loving, that Saint Francis said that if the experience had lasted longer, his life would have melted away in joy.

Compared to this experience, all the pleasures of the world become insignificant. Even the most elevated artistic experiences cannot be compared with the boundless joy and love we feel in this supreme state. One taste of it, even for a moment, and you will want to make it last forever.

That is why I tell everyone to make meditation their first priority. No time could be better spent. I led a very busy life when I began to meditate many decades ago, and I still lead a busy life, but I have always found time to meditate. You can be sure that when you make meditation your first priority, you will enjoy the benefits from it every day.

Even after decades of meditation I still cannot get over the miracle of what precious treasures lie within our consciousness, ready to be discovered through the practice of this simple discipline. Every morning as I finish my meditation, I realize anew how immensely it can enrich our lives and the lives of those around us.

I think it is important for everybody to learn to meditate. Anybody who wants to be healthy – which means everybody – needs to meditate. Anybody who wants a calm mind and a loving heart – which again means everybody – needs to meditate. One of the greatest benefits of meditation is the loss of any feeling of inadequacy you may have. It is amazing to me, but I don't ever feel inadequate today. I don't know what the meaning of depression is. I have many important responsibilities, many challenges come up every day, but I know that I can dive deep into my consciousness in meditation and bring up with me the resources necessary for dealing with any dilemma the day may bring.

I was not born this way. It is something that I achieved through long years of discipline and the grace of my teacher, my grandmother. And when this state is achieved, a great teacher of meditation in ancient India makes this quiet statement: "Now you see yourself as you really are."

Before I took to meditation, although I was leading a satisfactory and successful life, I didn't have any idea of who I am. Of course, I thought I knew: I was a village boy from Kerala who had become professor of English on a campus in Central India and was sure he was enjoying life and perhaps even contributing to it a little. Only later did I realize that I had been asleep and dreaming – no more awake, as William James says, than a man who thinks his capacities are limited to what he can do with his little finger.

One inspired verse in the Indian scriptures defines clearly who we are:

> When the wise realize the Self,
> Formless in the midst of forms, changeless
> In the midst of change, omnipresent
> And supreme, they go beyond sorrow.

The beauty and wisdom of these words is unsurpassed. They express the summit of human wisdom, because they tell us who we are. They say, in the simplest possible language, that within this physical, changing, mortal body there is a nonphysical presence which is our true Self.

When I was enabled, after years of meditation, to discover who I am, the joy of that discovery knew no bounds. And my love knew – and knows – no bounds. Today I know I am not just a separate fragment of existence subject to old age and death. I live in everyone. I am related to everything around me – the seas, the skies, the mountains, the rivers, the forests, the beasts of the field and the birds of the air. I am an immortal being with a million interconnections with all of life. This is our greatness, to be connected with everything on earth. And when we discover this, the Buddha says, we go beyond all sorrow.

Ideas and Suggestions

Spiritual Reading All of us need daily inspiration to remind us of the higher meaning and purpose of our lives. I recommend half an hour or so each day for reading from the scriptures and the writings of the great mystics of all religions. (See page 157)

Mantram Repetition Choose a mantram that appeals to you deeply and try it for at least a month, following the instructions and guidelines on page 196.

Meditation Set aside half an hour every morning for meditation, as early as is convenient. Instructions in passage meditation begin on page 194.

CHAPTER 8

The Still Center

When the mind grows still,
it is full of healing power.

One of my delights as a professor of English literature was to introduce Shakespeare to a freshman class. In every final I gave, however, I found that my students almost never told me what they themselves thought about Shakespeare. They gave me only quotations from the experts. "Don't tell me what the experts say about the play," I would insist. "I've read the experts. I want to know what you have learned, what this play means to you."

That is one of the reasons I refer to Mahatma Gandhi so often. When Gandhi wrote or said something, it was always based on direct, personal experience. This overriding practicality is one of the marks of genuine spiritual experience. Gandhi did not spend time theorizing and philosophizing. He would always say, "Why not learn by getting down to the actual practice?"

Sri Ramakrishna, a great nineteenth-century Bengali

mystic, used to say similarly, "When you go to a mango tree,
you don't go to count the leaves. Get up into the tree, pluck a
mango, and eat it; then you will know about mangoes." When it
comes to the benefits of stilling the mind, there is no substitute
for giving it a try and tasting the fruits of it ourselves.

> All of us have moments when we forget
> time completely. It is in those moments
> that we experience happiness.

Until we have this experience for ourselves, however, we need
to fall back on metaphors and illustrations. All of us have
moments when we forget the passage of time completely – usually when we are intently absorbed in doing something we like.

In my early days in this country, a friend of mine took me
to see American football, which is entirely different from what
we called football in India (you call it soccer). There was a big
crowd, and a lot of excitement when those figures dressed in
primeval costumes and looking like supermen came onto the
field. My friend was a good commentator, and he carefully
explained to me the system of scoring and some of the rules
of the game. But during the second half of the match he got
so completely absorbed that he stopped talking to me. Then,
suddenly, one side scored a touchdown. My friend – usually

a rather reserved person – jumped up and fell upon the man seated in front, squashing his hat on his head. I told him later, "You not only forgot yourself, but you forgot the poor fellow seated in front of you, too!"

Whether we are aware of it or not, all of us are capable of these moments of utter self-forgetfulness, and it is in these moments that we experience happiness. You can see why I call it a tragedy that we are bombarded with propaganda that tells us to dwell on the body as the source of joy, for joy is to be found in just the opposite direction.

In the deepest stages of meditation, the mind gradually comes to a temporary stop. This is the state that Zen Buddhism calls "no mind." It sounds negative, but this is a tremendous experience. Afterwards, you realize that if your body is like a car you drive, your mind is the engine. You are not your mind; you are the driver – which means, among other things, that you know how to slow down your car when you like and even how to park it, put the engine in neutral, turn it off, and put the key in your pocket. Most of the time, without realizing it, we leave the mind idling on the street with the key still in the ignition, where it wastes gas and pollutes the air until some vagrant thought drives off with it.

This mind of ours is constantly chugging away, even when it is doing nothing. To be able to turn it off and let it rest without thought is to be in heaven. To have a still mind means there is a healing silence everywhere. In this supreme state, you are absolutely fulfilled. You don't need anything outside yourself. You don't need to manipulate other people. You don't need to accumulate material possessions. You don't need to depend upon any of the unreliable props that modern civilization produces.

This experience may last just for a few moments, for the twinkling of an eye. But once you taste this experience, you realize how paltry all the satisfactions of the external world are.

People often ask me, "How would you compare your life today with your life before you took to meditation?" I don't come from a poor family, so I don't answer as someone who was ever deprived. In fact, I come from an affluent, cultured family that has produced leaders, scholars, and artists in my part of Kerala for centuries. I had a good education and was able to pursue the careers I wanted as a university professor and writer. And I enjoyed my work very much. By Indian standards, I was quite successful. I had no frustrations – in fact, I was a happy man. Yet today there is no comparison. Today my life is a million times better. Not just better, a million times better.

Until we experience this state ourselves, it is not possible to understand it. But once you get a taste of the love and the joy of it, you will want to live in this state permanently.

> As the thinking process slows
> down, you can see your mind with
> detachment and learn to tune it just as
> a mechanic tunes a performance car.

In the spring, when the weather is beautiful and the hills of California are green with new grass, I sometimes go for a joyride
in the afternoon with a few friends. I always say to the driver,
"Don't go fast. I like to look at all the cows and calves, the sheep
and lambs, the deer, the wildflowers on the hills."

This is very much like what happens in your mind as
your thinking process slows down. Then you are able to see
thoughts with some detachment. You can see them gamboling
like lambs on the hillside, and if they are playful and beautiful
like the lambs, you can enjoy them. You can see even the small,
tender thoughts that grow like wildflowers in out-of-the-way
places. Life becomes most enjoyable.

Of course, unpleasant situations still come. No one can
avoid them. But when your mind is still, instead of getting agitated in an unpleasant situation, you can see the other person's
point of view, understand why he is agitated, and do something
to calm him down – even if you have to oppose him tenderly
but resolutely.

When you get this kind of detachment from your mind, you
can look at its workings much as a watchmaker looks at the

inside of a watch. When a watch is going too fast, the watch-maker doesn't throw it away. He opens it, loosens a wire or screw, and gets the machinery to go a little slower.

I had a friend who was very good at this. I used to be amazed when she would put on her magnifying glass, open my watch, look at what was hidden behind the case, and then make a few little adjustments so that the watch kept perfect time.

Similarly, after years of training, I have learned to do this with my mind. I can look at it with detachment, open it up, and see what is going on. It's a very interesting spectacle. If you know how to open your mind at the back like this, you will see to your amazement that your mind is not you; it is a process.

This is such a simple statement, but it may take a lifetime to understand and practice it. You can look inside your mind and see for yourself that in order to get angry, your mind has to speed up. To hold on to a resentment, thoughts have to keep racing around. You can actually observe the process by which the mind speeds up, and then you are able to slow it down and set it right. It means that you are not an angry person or a resentful person; you simply have a watch that goes too fast, which can be adjusted.

Once you have gained this marvelous skill, you will be able to set the speed of the mind at the rate you like. You will gain the capacity, when anger comes, to slow it down and turn it into compassion. This simple adjustment in the speed of thought is actually all that is required to transform the explosive energy of anger into the deep reserves of power that are compassion.

> The healing stillness of a quiet mind
> nourishes every aspect of our lives.

If you have been practicing meditation sincerely and systematically, the day has to come when you enter the still center within. Then you don't hear the cars on the road outside or the music next door. All your attention is focused within, and your mind slows down almost to a crawl.

This reminds me of a story I heard about Lyndon Johnson. In the course of campaigning, it is said, he was telling some small farmers that he understood their needs because he was a rancher himself.

One man asked, "How big is your spread?"

"It's *big*," Johnson replied in his best Texan manner. "I get in my car in the morning, and it's sunset before I cross my own property line."

Like most farmers, this man knew politicians. "Yeah," he said, "I had that kind of car once too."

That kind of car may not be the best for inspecting a Texas ranch, but that kind of mind is excellent. Only when the mind isn't speeding can we see that there is actually an interval between one thought and another – an interval in which there is actually no thought going on at all.

This state of "no mind" is so beneficial to body and mind, so revealing of the nature of life, that once you discover it, you become unshakably secure. You know that even if something terribly upsetting happens – a bereavement, a dismissal from your job, an attack, a financial loss – you have only to enter that interval where there is no thought and rest there. You can sit down for meditation with no movement in the mind and come back refreshed, renewed, and whole.

That is why the Buddha says, "Not your parents, not your partner, not your best friends can bring you such peace as a well-trained mind." The Bible calls this "the peace that passes all understanding." You alone can find this peace for yourself, for it lies in the depths of your own consciousness. All of us are human enough to want to be comforted, and we often feel we need consolation from others. But the Buddha reminds us that although others can wipe away our tears and comfort us, who can heal the wounds of the mind? How can anyone reach the pain inside? There we have to be our own healer; no one else can do this for us. We need the deep healing that comes from a mind at peace.

Between one thought and the next
is a tiny gap when the mind is at peace.
Extending that gap is the secret of an
unhurried mind.

This gap of stillness between one thought and another is our safety. While driving, I am told, there should be one car length between cars for every ten miles per hour of speed. When you are going fifty miles per hour, for example, safe driving demands that you maintain the distance of five car lengths between your car and the car in front.

Similarly, I would say, we can learn not to let one thought tailgate another. Tailgating thoughts are a danger signal. People who are prone to anger – or to fear, or greed, or hostility – allow no distance between one thought and another, between one emotional reaction and the next. Their anger seems continuous – just one anger car after another, bumping into each other on a fast, crowded highway.

When a person is like this, we are likely to say, "Better not go near him! He's an angry person." Prudently, we keep our distance. But I don't avoid angry people today. In fact, I am often able to help them because I don't see anger as a continuous phenomenon. I see it as little bursts of anger: one burst, then another, then a third, a fourth, a fifth. When you are getting angry, if you could only slow your mind down a little, you would be able to see that between one angry thought and the next there is actually no connection at all.

That is one reason the mantram can be of such help. When you repeat the mantram when you are angry, you are inserting it between angry thoughts and pushing them apart. The mantram acts like a traffic cop: "Okay, break it up!" Your thoughts slow down, and you begin to see things more clearly and understand what is the best action to take.

A person whose mind is slow lives in a wonderful world. He can cause nobody any harm; she can cause herself no harm. There is a sign in such a person's mind to slow down traffic: "Go Slow, Children Playing."

Too often, the situation is very different. We need a sign that says, "Caution, Adults Angry." When adults are bursting out in anger, you need to be awfully careful. But when your own mind is slow, you will be calm under attack. You will be in control of your own responses. Then you will not be afraid of angry people; you will be able to face them with affection in your heart, security in your mind, and a quiet confidence that you can slow down their anger. Even a belligerent person can sense that you are remaining calm, so you not only remain free from anger yourself but help the other person to calm down too.

We are told that the mind and body are geared for either fight or flight. But there is a third alternative: we can face a difficult situation calmly, with compassion.

Mahatma Gandhi, who called himself a practical idealist, said that he wanted to live in peace not only with his friends, but with his enemies also. He knew that there were people who disliked him and opposed him, but he wanted to be able to love and respect them.

This is a sound approach to life. When you allow yourself to dislike someone, *your* peace is disturbed – not their peace of mind but your own. Tragically, we are bound to those people we dislike and shackled to those whom we hate.

It is essential to be able to slow down the mind enough that we don't have an automatic negative response when facing criticism. If we want sound health and unshakable security, we have to learn to be loving and calm under all circumstances. We have to learn to be as concerned about the welfare of those who dislike us as we are for those who like us. And we have to be the same whether people respect us or censure us. A fast mind cannot do these things. But with a slow, calm mind, you can move into any situation, ready for anything.

> We all need the protection
> of a mind at peace.

We all need the protection of a patient, unhurried, well-trained mind. If life were always pleasant, it wouldn't matter so much if our minds were speeding out of control. But life has a way of presenting us with speed bumps. If you hit a speed bump at seventy miles per hour, you are going to be in the hospital. When life puts up speed bumps, we have to be able to slow down to get over them without injury.

Here is where you can use all the strategies I have given in the preceding chapters. When life throws up an obstacle – say, a problem that is getting unpleasant – don't swell it with your attention. Put your attention fully on your work, work hard without thinking about yourself, and repeat your mantram in your mind whenever you can to keep hold of the center of stillness you tapped in the morning's meditation. This simple strategy can keep your mind from speeding up under the pressure of any problem. At the end of the day, you will find that your problems have been reduced to a manageable size. Remember, problems have a way of swelling when we feed them with our attention; when they are starved for attention, they shrink or even go away.

These are valuable skills, which can free us not only from useless worry about today's problems but from old memories and resentments as well. Older people particularly need these skills. It is sad to listen to older people talk vividly about events that happened ten years ago – often, as the Buddha says, about how someone abused them, someone injured them, someone robbed them. In people who dwell on such thoughts, the Buddha says, hatred, anger, and resentment can never cease.

Through years of practice I have trained my mind not to dwell on those thoughts, and as a result, they don't come to me. Gandhi said that this can go to such an extent that thoughts like these do not come even in our dreams.

This strategy is particularly important in safeguarding ourselves from the suffering caused by negative emotions like depression, dejection, despondency, inadequacy, and guilt. Guilt, in particular, is one of the most burdensome banes of modern life. But it is only one more of the many tricks the mind uses to get us to dwell on ourselves. You will never get bored studying your mind. It always comes up with surprises, and one of the most unpleasant of these surprises is guilt. The mind starts singing its refrain – "How terrible you were that day! You should be ashamed of yourself! Don't you feel embarrassed when you think about what you did?" And we fall in: "Oh, yes!"

At these times, the mind is only playing one of its favorite tapes. Imagine buying a new sound system, setting it up, and arranging your speakers to get the acoustics perfect; then you take out this old tape full of hiss and static and sit down happily to listen to the same old tired recording! Not only that, but you set it to automatically repeat itself whenever it reaches the end.

The first or second time, there may be a purpose in listening to this tape if it enables us to learn from some past mistake. But the tragedy of getting caught in a guilt complex is that we go on helplessly sitting there listening to this debilitating message as if to immerse ourselves in thoughts of how bad we are. When the mind plays what it likes, that is all we can do. But what a relief just to be able to reach over, press the Stop button, and give our mind a rest.

A mind at peace is naturally full of love.

Every human heart has a deep need to love – to be in love, really, with all of life. This is the kind of love that comes when the mind is still.

In this sense, Romeo and Juliet are in preschool as far as love goes. Men and women like Francis of Assisi and Teresa of Avila are the ones who truly know what love means.

I wish I could convey to you the endless romance of this love that flows from the still mind. If you can find joy in being in love with one person, isn't the joy a millionfold greater if you can be in love with all?

When I travel on the freeways I see stickers that say "I love my dog," "I love my cat," "I love New York." If I were ever to put a sticker on my car, it would simply say "I love." That is our human legacy, which we claim when the mind is stilled. This is what the Bible means when it says, "Be still and know that I am God." Be still and know that we are all God's children; then you will be in love with all.

You don't know what real love is until you love all. When the mind is still, you see everybody as your own self. You see every country as your own. You will not be capable of harming anybody, even if they have harmed or hurt you; you will help even those who harm you. That is the nature of the love that flows from the hearts of people like Saint Francis and Gandhi.

All of us need this universal love, and all of us are looking for it – but we look for it somewhere outside. We don't know that it can be found within, at the still center within the heart.

> A still mind brings the infinite joy and
> love for which we were born.

When the mind is stilled, it is like crossing the timberline on a mountain peak. Mountain climbers will tell you that beyond a certain elevation no trees can grow. When the mind is stilled, no fragmentary, fraudulent thoughts can grow: no selfish urges, no resentments, no hostilities. All those who have become established in this state say on the basis of their personal experience that this is infinite joy and infinite love, for which all of us are born.

Great geniuses in fields like poetry, science, and music have experienced recurring periods of this stillness of the mind. Einstein recognized this when he said that the highest mode of knowing is the mystical. But while scientists and artists experience only fleeting glimpses of this stillness, it is men and women of God who are established in it always. They take a little of that healing stillness with them wherever they go.

In my lifetime, I have been privileged to have seen several such men and women in India. One of them, Swami Ramdas, tells us on the strength of his own experience that we can never know what real joy is until the mind is still. Until then, he says, we are simply picking up a few crumbs of pleasure and trying to convince ourselves that it is joy.

We are not here to walk about pecking at crumbs like pigeons, Ramdas says. It is our destiny to fly. Not just the fortunate few, but every one of us has been born to soar. And until we do, we can find no lasting peace anywhere. In a different simile, Ramdas tells us that "the river of life struggles through all obstacles and conditions to reach the vast and infinite ocean of existence who is God. . . . It knows no rest, no freedom, and no peace until it mingles with the waters of immortality and delights in the visions of infinity."

Similarly, Mechthild of Magdeburg, a Western mystic of the thirteenth century, described in beautiful poetry the immense benefits that flow from a mind at rest and a heart full of love. This is neither theory nor metaphysics, but a record of her own personal experience:

"Of the heavenly things God has taught me, I can speak but a little word, not more than a honeybee can carry away on its feet from an overflowing jar. . . . In the first choir is happiness, the highest of all gifts. In the second, gentleness. In the third, loving-kindness. In the fourth, sweetness. In the fifth, joyfulness. In the sixth, honorable rest. In the seventh, riches. In the eighth, merit. In the ninth, fervent love."

I particularly like this phrase "honorable rest." Mechthild is being very careful about her phraseology. She says not just "rest" but "honorable rest": that is, resting at the center while contributing to life in full measure. When your mind is still, you can work hard and be active every day of your life and still be at rest, because you will not be working under the goad of personal ambition. That's the secret of Gandhi, who worked for a selfless cause fifteen hours a day seven days a week even in his seventies but never got exhausted, because, he said, "I am always at rest."

> We are not here to peck at crumbs like
> pigeons. We are born to soar in
> freedom with a mind at peace and a
> heart full of love.

Many years ago our friend Mary asked Christine and me if we would like to go to Yosemite. "I think you will enjoy camping," she said. "The mountains are beautiful this time of year."

I was expecting a wilderness, so I was astonished to see

hordes of people in a crowded campground. In fact, throughout that day we didn't see much but cars and campers. "Why
come to Yosemite," I wondered, "when you can see all this in
Berkeley?"

But that night, when people had finally gone to sleep and
the cars and radios were silent, I emerged from my meditation to hear a little brook warbling past the tent, singing its
song: *Rama, Rama, Rama* . . . "Where was this brook during
the day?" I wondered. "Wasn't it here then?" It had been there,
of course; we simply hadn't been aware of it. People, cars, and
radios had drowned its sweet voice in their racket. Only when
all of this had fallen silent could we hear the gentle, soothing
sound of its music.

It is the same with the mind. As long as it is blaring as usual,
we cannot hear the "still, small voice" inside. Meditation is for
the purpose of quieting the tumult of the mind, so that, after a
long, long period, when this cacophony has been brought to
an unregretted end, we hear the healing silence that has been
going on within us all the time.

When we can rest our mind at will, still our mind at will, we
live in a world that is one. Today we don't see the world as it is;
we see only conflict, separateness, and ceaseless change. As the
Bible says, we see "as through a glass darkly," because we look
through the distorting glass of a hurried mind – a mind subject
to the fog of anger, fear, greed, and all the other negative emo-

tions that are part of the human condition. As William Blake says, "When the doors of perception are cleansed, everything appears as it is, infinite."

You and I, when the mind is still, see that the mountains and the seas, the forests and the rivers, the animals and the birds, the trees and the plants, all nations, all races, all men and women and children, are one. Once you see this in the silence of your heart, you will never be the same person again. You will return from this summit of spiritual awareness full of practical wisdom, passionate love, and untiring energy which you will want to use for the benefit of all.

Passage Meditation:
An Eight-Point Program

The Eight Point Program: An Overview

1. Meditation on a Passage Silent repetition in the mind of memorized inspirational passages from the world's great religions. Practiced for one-half hour each morning.

2. Repetition of a Mantram Silent repetition in the mind of a Holy Name or a hallowed phrase from one of the world's great religions. Practiced whenever possible throughout the day or night.

3. Slowing Down Setting priorities and reducing the stress and friction caused by hurry.

4. One-Pointed Attention Giving full concentration to the matter at hand.

5. Training the Senses Overcoming conditioned habits and learning to enjoy what is beneficial.

6. Putting Others First Gaining freedom from selfishness and separateness; finding joy in helping others.

7. Spiritual Fellowship Spending time regularly with other passage meditators for mutual inspiration and support.

8. Spiritual Reading Drawing inspiration from writings by and about the world's great spiritual figures and from the scriptures of all religions.

Meditation & Related Skills

Slowing down, as I have presented it in this book, is one of the points in the Eight Point Program I have developed and followed myself for a fuller, healthier, more spiritual life. The other points have been touched on in this book as well. If you are interested in the full program, you will find a summary on the opposite page. Each point is explained in detail in my book *Passage Meditation* and at www.bmcm.org.

When this Eight Point Program is followed daily to the best of one's ability, as I can testify from my own personal experience, it is possible for everyone to lead a secure, healthy, selfless life. Even a little such practice will begin to transform your life, leading to profoundly beneficial changes in yourself and the world around you.

If you'd like to get started with meditation or the mantram right away, here are my instructions :

How to Meditate

The heart of this program is meditation. The principle of meditation is simple: we are what we think. When we meditate on inspired words with profound concentration, they have the capacity to sink into our consciousness, alive with a charge of spiritual awareness. Eventually these ideals become an integral part of our personality, which means they will find constant expression in what we do, what we say, and what we think.

Half an hour every morning, as early as is convenient, is the best time for meditation. Do not increase this period; if you want to meditate more, have half an hour in the evening also, preferably at the very end of the day.

Set aside a special place to be used only for meditation and spiritual reading. After a while that place will become associated with meditation in your mind, so that simply entering it will have a calming effect. If you cannot spare a room, have a particular corner. Whichever you choose, keep your meditation place clean, well ventilated, and reasonably austere.

Sit in a straight-backed chair or on the floor and gently close your eyes. If you sit on the floor, you may need to support your back lightly against a wall. You should be comfortable enough to forget your body, but not so comfortable that you become drowsy.

Whatever position you choose, be sure to keep your head, neck, and spinal column erect in a straight line. As concentration deepens, the nervous system relaxes and you may begin to fall asleep. It is important to resist this tendency right from the beginning by drawing yourself up and away from your back support until the wave of sleep has passed.

Once you have closed your eyes, begin to go slowly, in your mind, through one of the passages from the scriptures or the great mystics that I recommend for use in meditation. I usually suggest learning first the Prayer of Saint Francis of Assisi (*see page 161*). As you go through the prayer, let each word sink like a jewel into your consciousness.

In memorizing the prayer, it may be helpful to remind yourself that you are not addressing some being outside you. The kingdom of heaven is within us, and in this prayer we are calling deep into ourselves, appealing to the spark of the divine that is our real nature.

While you are meditating, do not follow any association of ideas or try to think about the passage. If you are giving your attention to each word, the meaning cannot help sinking in. When distractions come, do not resist them, but give more attention to the words of the passage. If your mind strays from the passage entirely, bring it back gently to the beginning and start again.

When you reach the end of the passage, you may use it again as necessary to complete your period of meditation until you have memorized others. It is helpful to have a wide variety of passages for meditation, drawn from the world's major spiritual traditions. Each passage should be positive and practical, selected from a major scripture or a mystic of the highest stature. Many beautiful passages selected from the world's great spiritual traditions can be found in my collection *God Makes the Rivers to Flow*, as well as on the Web at www.bmcm.org/passages.

How to Use a Mantram

Every major religion has a mantram, often more than one. If you have no affiliation with a religion, however, you can still use a mantram and benefit from it. I have heard countless times from confirmed skeptics and agnostics that the mantram came to their help just when they needed it, though they hadn't expected it to mean anything to them at all.

One of the oldest and most popular mantrams in India, *Rama,* is the one Mahatma Gandhi used. *Rama* (the word rhymes with *drama*) is a name of the Lord that comes from a word meaning "joy" or "to rejoice," so repeating *Rama, Rama, Rama* is calling on the source of joy in our hearts. When someone comes to me for a mantram and says that he or she doesn't believe in God or belong to any particular religion, this is the mantram I most often give them. It is short, rhythmic, easy to remember, and powerful.

Another mantram I often give is the Buddhist phrase *Om mani padme hum*. *Mani* means "jewel" and *padme* "lotus"; together the words refer to "the jewel in the lotus of the heart." This mantram simply means that the Buddha-nature, a jewel beyond price, is present in every heart.

The Catholic tradition has a beautiful mantram in the simple words *Ave Maria*. In the Eastern Orthodox traditions, variations of the Jesus Prayer – "Lord, Jesus Christ, have mercy on us," or simply *Kyrie eleison* – have been used for centuries. And for Christians of all traditions, the very name of Jesus is one of the oldest mantrams of all.

Similarly, in Islam, the name of Allah itself is a mantram. Another is *Bismillah ir-Rahman ir-Rahim*: "In the name of God, the Compassionate, the Merciful." Jews may repeat the familiar *Barukh attah Adonai* – "Blessed art thou, O Lord" – or a revered formula used as a mantram by the Hasidim: *Ribono shel olam,* "Lord of the universe."

Select your mantram carefully. Please don't make up your own; use one that has been sanctified by tradition, as have all the ones I recommend here. Then, once you have chosen, stick to it. Don't try one for a while and then change to another. If you do, you will be like a person who keeps digging wells in many places; you will never strike water.

Whatever mantram you choose, repeat it to yourself silently, in the mind, whenever you find yourself getting agitated or speeded up. That is when you will discover its power. When you have a quarrel with somebody at work, for example, you have to deal with the situation somehow, so what do you do? No amount of telling yourself "I really shouldn't get angry over this little incident" is likely to slow down a mind that is already in turmoil. That is the time to use one of the simplest strategies taught in all great spiritual traditions. Instead of reacting with hostility or sitting in silence while your mind seethes with anger, simply repeat your mantram silently until you feel calm again.

This is particularly effective when you can combine it with a good, fast walk. Just a turn around the block or up and down a flight of stairs helps greatly. This is one of the easiest methods of reducing the speed of the mind. There is a close connection between the rhythm of the mantram, the rhythm of the footstep, the rhythm of breathing, and the rhythm of the mind.

Use your mantram as much as possible – silently, in the mind – whenever you find an opportunity: while waiting in line, while doing mechanical tasks like washing dishes, and especially while falling asleep at night. Practice – diligent, determined practice – is what counts with the repetition of the mantram. At first the repetition may seem mechanical, but every repetition takes you a little deeper. Gandhi used to say it's like walking: each step is like all the others, but you are moving forward with every stride.

Of course, when you are doing a job that requires attention, you should not try to use the mantram. That is the time to give your complete attention to the job. Most work requires this kind of attention. When operating a piece of machinery, one-pointed attention is not just training the mind; it is vital for safety. (Driving, incidentally, is operating a particularly dangerous piece of machinery.) These are not times for the mantram.

However, there are many, many occasions during the day when the mind is not actively engaged in a one-pointed task, and those are just the times when it tends to get caught in old, compulsive habits – worry, resentment, insecurity, gossip, replaying old recordings from the past. These are all times to use the mantram instead.

You can use the mantram to invigorate the mind when you are getting bored, and to overcome inertia when you feel physically or mentally stale. And you can use it to control restlessness when the mind is speeding up. The mantram is an indispensable tool that I recommend to anyone who wants to find peace in a world of stress and hurry.

Index

jobs, *see* work
Johnson, Lyndon, 177
joy, clinging to, 103–4
judgment: and discrimination, 87, 96;
    and likes and dislikes, 116, 117

Kerala, India, *see* India
Kyrie eleison, 197

lateness, *see* punctuality
likes and dislikes: becoming less
    rigid, 106, 107, 109–10, 116;
    of children, 110–11; and
    food, 110–13; as habits of
    mind, 105, 112–14; rigidity of,
    104–7; sensory, loosening,
    116–18; vs. values, 107–9
listening, 109, 141; and one-
    pointed attention, 65–67
living in present, 7–9, 34,
    61–62, 79, 98, 104
living intentionally: slowing
    down as means to, 54
love: and patience, 50, 140;
    real, 184–85; *see also*
    personal relationships
loyalty: and one-pointed attention, 75

magazines, *see* media
mantram: choices for, 196–97; effect
    on anger, 180; as element of
    Eight Point Program, 192, 196–
    99; vs. meditation, 160–61; and
    religion, 158; slowing down
    mind with, 158–60; and walking,
    198; when not to use, 199;
    when to use, 160, 161, 197–99

mealtimes: and children, 110; and
    companionship, 46; doing
    something else while eating,
    63–64; *see also* breakfast
Mechthild of Magdeburg, 186–87
media, 42, 145–46, 154; *see also*
    television
meditation: attention during, 162, 165;
    benefits of, 165–68; best time for,
    160, 193; choosing passages for,
    160–61, 163; deepest stages of,
    165–68, 173, 177–79; difficulty of,
    162; Easwaran turns to, 34–35; as
    element of Eight Point Program,
    192, 193–96; how to sit, 194–
    95; length of time for, 194; vs.
    mantram, 160–61; places for, 194;
    and posture, 194–95; sleepiness
    in, 195; slowing down mind
    with, 160–68; teaching of, 162
mental blocks, 89–90
mind: automobile analogies, 58–59,
    60, 70; changing channels in,
    76–77; and consciousness,
    122; detachment from, 175–
    76; Easwaran as personal
    trainer, 11; effect of one-
    pointed attention, 60–61; fast
    vs. slow vs. still, 52; and food,
    111–13; impact of anger on, 53,
    179–80; during meditation,
    162, 165; one-pointed, 70–71;
    racing, 53, 148, 149, 159–60;
    and rigid habits, 105, 112–15;
    role of experience in shaping,
    108–9; slowing down, 52–54;
    slowing with mantram, 158–

60; slowing with meditation, 160, 162; still, 52, 96, 118, 171–89; television analogy, 52–53; untrained, 53; well-trained, 76–79, 178, 181; *see also* attention

mindfulness, 73; *see also* attention, one-pointed; concentration

moment, living in, *see* living in present

morning: best time for meditation, 160, 193; and breakfast, 20, 41–42; importance of quiet time, 41, 157; setting day's pace, 20–21, 41

multitasking, 15; *see also* hurrying

My Fair Lady, 149

negative emotions: effect on mind and body, 53; vs. positive, 76, 148, 164–65; safeguarding against, 183–84; speed of, 53, 148, 179

New York: Easwaran in, 12, 37–38

newspapers, *see* media

"no mind" state, 173, 178

Om mani padme hum, 197

one-pointed attention, *see* attention, one-pointed

opposition, facing, 67–68

Orthodox tradition: and mantram, 197

pace of life: effect of getting up early, 40–41; as problem, 20–21; setting, 41; slowing down, 40–42; *see also* slowing down

past: training attention away from, 57–62, 104

Patanjali, 74

patience, 140, 143–44; cultivating, 50–52; as virtue, 15, 50

personal relationships: and automatic teller machines, 127–28; basis for, 139–44; with children, 47, 132; differences in, 139–44; difficult, 67, 68, 144–45, 179, 198; and entertainment, 135; as fundamental, 129; importance of, 131–33; likes and dislikes in, 109–10; and mealtimes, 46–47; one-pointed attention in, 66–67; putting others first, 145, 146,192; and spiritual companionship, 145, 192; taking time for, 46–47

pleasure: clinging to, 103–4; passing nature of, 119

postal system, 38–40, 133

Prayer of Saint Francis of Assisi, 160–61

present, living in, *see* living in present

pressure: on children, 44; contagiousness of, 40; *see also* speed

priorities: meditation as, 166; setting, 44–46; *see also* to-do lists

problems: feeding with attention, 165, 182; shrinking, 165, 182

punctuality: Gandhi's view, 30; and hurrying, 20–21; in India, 30; lack of, 20

putting others first: as element of Eight Point Program, 192; transforming influence of, 145; as visiting heaven, 146

quality time, 47

The Blue Mountain Center of Meditation

The Blue Mountain Center of Meditation publishes Eknath Easwaran's books, videos, and audio recordings, and offers retreats and online programs on passage meditation.

For more information and resources, please visit:

www.bmcm.org

The Blue Mountain Center of Meditation
Box 256, Tomales, California 94971

Telephone: +1 707 878 2369
Toll-free in the US: 800 475 2369

Email: info@bmcm.org

Passage Meditation – A Complete Spiritual Practice
Train Your Mind & Find a Life that Fulfills

Easwaran's classic manual is a unique source of practical spiritual support for new and experienced meditators, and gives all the instruction needed to establish a vibrant meditation practice and keep it going. In passage meditation, you focus attention on passages, or texts, drawn from all the world's sacred traditions. You choose the passages that appeal to you, so this universal method stays fresh and inspiring, prompting you to live out your highest ideals.

Easwaran taught passage meditation to thousands of people for over forty years, including a course at the University of California, Berkeley. Meditation is supported by the mantram and six other spiritual tools to help us stay calm, kind, and focused throughout the day. This book shows how, with regular practice, we gain wisdom and vitality, and find a life that fulfills.

The Mantram Handbook
A Practical Guide to Choosing Your Mantram
& Calming Your Mind

A mantram (or mantra) is a short, powerful spiritual formula or prayer word from the world's great traditions. Examples include *Rama, Rama,* used by Gandhi; *My God and My All,* used by Saint Francis of Assisi; and the Buddhist mantram, *Om mani padme hum.*

Easwaran explains how to choose a mantram, and shows through stories and examples how it can be repeated silently anytime, anywhere, to help calm the mind and access our deepest wisdom.

Repeat your chosen mantram when you are worried, angry, or caught in regrets, and it will guide and comfort you like a true friend.

God Makes the Rivers to Flow
An Anthology of the World's Sacred Poetry & Prose

Easwaran drew deep, enduring inspiration from the sacred literature of all traditions. The 149 texts in this anthology come from the much-loved saints, sages, and scriptures of the Christian, Hindu, Sufi, Jewish, Native American, Buddhist, and Taoist traditions. These passages can be read for daily inspiration, for their insights into other spiritual traditions, for sustenance when we feel sad or tired, and for the deep transformation they can bring in Easwaran's method of passage meditation.

Rich supporting material includes detailed background notes, suggestions for memorization and for studying the texts in practices such as *lectio divina* from the Christian tradition, and instruction in passage meditation.

Strength in the Storm
Creating Calm in Difficult Times

We can't always control what life sends us, but we can choose how we respond, and that is largely a matter of quieting the agitation in the mind. It's a simple idea, but one that runs deep – a truly calm mind can weather any storm.

And we learn to calm the mind through practice – there's no magic about it. Easwaran offers insights, stories, practical techniques, and exercises that will help us release the wisdom we need to ride the waves of life minute by minute, day by day.

Conquest of Mind
Take Charge of Your Thoughts &
Reshape Your Life Through Meditation

Getting caught in unwanted thoughts and emotions can feel like an inevitable part of life. But Easwaran, who taught meditation for over forty years, shows a way to break free. Just as a fitness routine can result in a strong, supple body, spiritual disciplines can shape a secure personality and a resilient, loving mind.

Writing as an experienced, friendly coach, Easwaran explains how we can train the mind not just during meditation but throughout the day. Working with difficult colleagues, choosing what to eat, and listening to a child's needs are all opportunities to try out different, wiser responses.

To shed light on the thinking process, Easwaran takes the timeless teachings of the Buddha and other mystics and illustrates them with scenes from contemporary life. Training the mind is a great adventure, one that brings joy and purpose to life.

Gandhi the Man
How One Man Changed Himself to Change the World

Eknath Easwaran grew up in India and witnessed how Gandhi inspired people of all races, backgrounds, and religions to turn anger into compassion and hatred into love.

How had Gandhi done this? How had he transformed himself from an ineffective young lawyer into the Mahatma, the "great soul" who led 400 million Indians in their non-violent struggle for independence from the British Empire? To find out, Easwaran went to Gandhi's ashram and watched the Mahatma absorbed in meditation on the Bhagavad Gita, the wellspring of his spiritual strength.

Easwaran gives a moving account of the turning points and choices in Gandhi's life that made him not just a great political leader but also a timeless icon of nonviolence in every aspect of life.

This new edition includes over 70 digitally restored photographs, a detailed chronology with maps and notes, a new introduction by Easwaran, and an updated foreword by Michael Nagler, professor emeritus and cofounder of the Peace and Conflict Studies program, University of California, Berkeley.